Grade 1

Scott Foresman

Grammar and Writing Practice Book

PEARSON
Scott Foresman

Editorial Offices: Glenview, Illinois • Parsippany, New Jersey • New York, New York
Sales Offices: Needham, Massachusetts • Duluth, Georgia • Glenview, Illinois
Coppell, Texas • Sacramento, California • Mesa, Arizona

ISBN: 0-328-14622-6

2 3 4 5 6 7 8 9 10 V004 14 13 12 11 10 09 08 07 06 05

Unit 1 Animals, Tame and Wild

Unit 2 Communities

Unit 3 Changes

Grammar Extra Practice

Unit Writing Lessons

Sentences

A **sentence** is a group of words that tells a complete idea. It begins with a capital letter. Many sentences end with a period (.).

The cat is on a mat. ⟵ This is a sentence.
on a mat ⟵ This is not a sentence.

Find the sentence. **Write** the sentence.

1. Jim has a pet.   has a pet

_____
- -
_____

2. His pet   His pet is a cat.

_____
- -
_____

3. The cat   The cat runs away.

_____
- -
_____

4. Jim looks for his pet.   for his pet

_____
- -
_____

5. with Jim   We go with Jim.

_____
- -
_____

School-Home CONNECTION **Home Activity** Your child learned about sentences. Name an animal your child knows. Have your child say two sentences about the animal.

Sentences

Tell a story about when you did something with a pet.
Use some words from the box in your sentences.

| run | play | feed | watch |

_____

- -

_____

- -

_____

- -

_____

- -

_____

- -

_____

- -

© Pearson Education

Home Activity Your child learned how to use sentences in writing. Have your child write two sentences that tell about a pet your family has had.

Grammar and Writing Practice Book

Sentences

Mark the group of words that is a sentence.

I. ○ Ron gets a pet today.
   ○ a pet today
   ○ gets a pet

2. ○ a big cat
   ○ The pet is a big cat.
   ○ the pet

3. ○ plays with his
   ○ with his cat
   ○ Ron plays with his cat.

4. ○ He rolls the ball to the cat.
   ○ ball to the cat
   ○ rolls the ball to

5. ○ hits the ball
   ○ the ball back
   ○ The cat hits the ball back.

6. ○ and the cat like
   ○ Ron and the cat like the game.
   ○ Ron and the cat

Home Activity Your child prepared for taking tests on sentences. Read a story together. Have your child point out sentences in the story.

Sentences

Underline each sentence.

1. The girl feeds the cat.
   The girl

2. in a dish
   The food is in a dish.

3. The cat likes to eat.
   likes to eat

Finish each sentence. **Use** a group of words from the box.
Write the sentence.

have two pets.	two pets	The pets

_____

4. We _____

with the cat	plays with the cat.	Our dog

_____

5. The dog _____

Home Activity Your child reviewed sentences. Read aloud each group of words on the page. Ask your child whether or not each group is a sentence.

4 Unit 1 Week 1 **Day 5**

Grammar and Writing Practice Book

Name _____

Naming Parts of Sentences

A sentence has a **naming part.** It names a person, place, animal, or thing. The naming part tells who or what the sentence is about.

Pat sees a pig.   **The pig** is big.

↑   ↑

naming part   naming part

Write the naming part of each sentence.

1. My pig is sick.

2. A vet can help the pig.

3. We go to the vet.

4. The pig feels better.

5. My dad thanks the vet.

Home Activity Your child learned about the naming parts of sentences. Read a story together. Point to several sentences. Ask your child to identify the naming part of each sentence.

Grammar and Writing Practice Book   Unit 1 Week 2 **Day 2** **5**

© Pearson Education

Naming Parts of Sentences

Complete each sentence with a naming part.

_____
1. _____ is my favorite color.

_____
2. _____ is my favorite food.

_____
3. _____ is my favorite day.

Tell about things you like to do.

_____
_____
_____
_____
_____
_____
_____
_____

Home Activity Your child learned how to use naming parts of sentences in writing. Ask your child to underline the naming parts of the sentences he or she wrote on the page.

Naming Parts of Sentences

Mark the sentence that has a line under the naming part.

1. ○ My mom <u>is</u> a vet.
   ○ <u>My mom</u> is a vet.
   ○ My mom is <u>a vet</u>.

2. ○ <u>She</u> helps sick animals.
   ○ She <u>helps</u> sick animals.
   ○ She helps <u>sick animals</u>.

3. ○ That dog cut <u>its leg</u>.
   ○ That dog <u>cut</u> its leg.
   ○ <u>That dog</u> cut its leg.

4. ○ <u>This cat</u> hurt its paw.
   ○ This cat hurt <u>its paw</u>.
   ○ This cat <u>hurt</u> its paw.

5. ○ A vet will fix <u>them</u>.
   ○ <u>A vet</u> will fix them.
   ○ A vet <u>will</u> fix them.

6. ○ The animals <u>like</u> my mom.
   ○ The animals like <u>my</u> mom.
   ○ <u>The animals</u> like my mom.

Home Activity Your child prepared for taking tests on the naming parts of sentences. Write simple sentences about your family such as these: *Anne is your sister. Your mother works at a bank.* Ask your child to circle each naming part.

Name _____

Naming Parts of Sentences

Circle the naming part of each sentence.

1. Jan puts out food.

2. The dog eats too much!

3. My vet can help him.

Look at each picture. **Write** the naming part of each sentence.

The boy   We

_____

4. _____ plays the sax.

The girls   The pig

_____

5. _____ dances a jig.

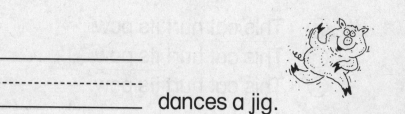

Maria   The cats

_____

6. _____ dances too.

Home Activity Your child reviewed naming parts of sentences. Have your child write on index cards the naming parts of the sentences on the page. Take turns choosing a card and using the naming part in a new sentence.

8 Unit 1 Week 2 **Day 5**

Grammar and Writing Practice Book

Action Parts of Sentences

A sentence has an **action part.** It tells what a person or thing does.

The ox **helps.**   He **pulls the wagon.**

    ↑   ↑

action part   action part

Write the action part of each sentence.

1. The cow gives milk.

_____

- - - - - - - - - - - - - - - - - - -

_____

2. Pop milks the cow.

_____

- - - - - - - - - - - - - - - - - - -

_____

3. The hen lays eggs.

_____

- - - - - - - - - - - - - - - - - - -

_____

4. Mom gets the eggs.

_____

- - - - - - - - - - - - - - - - - - -

_____

5. The cat chases mice.

_____

- - - - - - - - - - - - - - - - - - -

_____

Home Activity Your child learned about the action parts of sentences. Read a story together. Point to several sentences. Ask your child to identify the action part of each sentence.

Name _____

Action Parts of Sentences

Complete each sentence. **Write** an action part. **Tell** what the animal does.

1. A horse _____
_____

2. A duck _____
_____

3. A dog _____
_____

Tell about things that other animals do. Use words from the box or your own words.

| swims | jumps | hops | runs |

_____
_____
_____
_____
_____
_____

Home Activity Your child learned how to use action parts of sentences in writing. Ask your child to underline the action parts of the sentences he or she wrote on the page.

10 Unit 1 Week 3 **Day 3**

Grammar and Writing Practice Book

Name _____

Action Parts of Sentences

Mark the sentence that has a line under the action part.

1. ○ Ox gets a mop.
   ○ Ox gets a mop.
   ○ Ox gets a mop.

2. ○ He mops the pigs.
   ○ He mops the pigs.
   ○ He mops the pigs.

3. ○ Mom and Pop ride on Ox.
   ○ Mom and Pop ride on Ox.
   ○ Mom and Pop ride on Ox.

4. ○ Ox gets the cans.
   ○ Ox gets the cans.
   ○ Ox gets the cans.

5. ○ He packs the sack.
   ○ He packs the sack.
   ○ He packs the sack.

6. ○ They take a nap.
   ○ They take a nap.
   ○ They take a nap.

© Pearson Education

School-Home CONNECTION

Home Activity Your child prepared for taking tests on the action parts of sentences. Write simple sentences about your family such as these: *Bill plays football. Your sister feeds the baby.* Ask your child to circle each action part.

Action Parts of Sentences

Circle the action part of each sentence.

1. Nat rides the horse.

2. Mom feeds the ducks.

3. The girl walks her dog.

Look at each picture. **Write** the action part of each sentence.

runs   sleeps

4. The cat _____.

sings   flies

5. The bird _____.

swims   eats

6. The dog _____.

School-Home CONNECTION

Home Activity Your child reviewed action parts of sentences. Have your child write on index cards the action parts of the sentences on the page. Take turns choosing a card and using the action part in a new sentence.

© Pearson Education

Word Order

The **order** of the words in a sentence must make sense.

Zoo is at the Ned. ← These words are not in the right order.

Ned is at the zoo. ← These words are in the right order.

Circle the words that are in the right order.

1. Ned sees a fox.

   A sees fox Ned.

2. Kit the has fox a.

   The fox has a kit.

3. The kit naps on the rocks.

   The rocks naps on the kit.

4. The fox and the kit play.

   Kit the play fox the and.

5. Foxes the likes Ned.

   Ned likes the foxes.

© Pearson Education

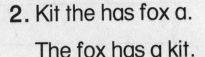

Home Activity Your child learned about word order in sentences. Help your child find several short simple sentences in a familiar story. Write each word in the sentences on an index card. Mix the cards for one sentence and have your child put the words in the correct order.

Word Order

Pretend you are one of the children in this picture.
Write a story about what you are doing at the zoo.
Make sure words are in the right order.

_____

- - - - - - - - - - - - - - -

_____

- - - - - - - - - - - - - - -

_____

- - - - - - - - - - - - - - -

_____

- - - - - - - - - - - - - - -

_____

- - - - - - - - - - - - - - -

_____

- - - - - - - - - - - - - - -

_____

Home Activity Your child learned how to use word order when writing sentences. Using several of your child's sentences, write them in scrambled order. Ask your child to tell you the right order of the words in each sentence.

Word Order

Mark the group of words that is in the correct order.

1. ○ Big zoo the is.
   ○ The zoo is big.
   ○ Is zoo big the.

2. ○ The zoo has many animals.
   ○ Animals has many zoo the.
   ○ Many has zoo the animals.

3. ○ Sees lions three Jan.
   ○ Three sees Jan lions.
   ○ Jan sees three lions.

4. ○ Lions sleep in the sun.
   ○ In sun sleep lions the.
   ○ Sleep lions sun in the.

5. ○ Watches seals the Hal.
   ○ Seals Hal the watches.
   ○ Hal watches the seals.

6. ○ With the seals a play ball.
   ○ The seals play with a ball.
   ○ Play the seals with ball a.

Home Activity Your child prepared for taking tests on word order in sentences. Read aloud each set of word groups on the page. Ask your child which group of words is in the right order.

Word Order

Underline the words that are in the right order.

1. Pat is at the zoo.

   The zoo at is Pat.

2. Zoo live at the animals.

   Animals live at the zoo.

3. Pat sees the animals.

   Animals sees the Pat.

Write the words so they are in the right order.
End each sentence with a period.

4. Apes a feeds the man.

   _____

   -

   _____

5. In food pan is the.

   _____

   -

   _____

6. Grab fruit they the.

   _____

   -

   _____

Home Activity Your child reviewed word order in sentences. Help your child write several simple sentences, each one on a strip of paper. Cut apart the words on each strip. Mix the pieces for each sentence and have your child put the words in the correct order.

Name _____

Telling Sentences

A **telling sentence** tells something. It is a statement. It begins with a **capital letter**. It usually ends with a **period (.)**.

The bird has a nest.
The nest is in a tree.

Find the sentence. **Underline** the sentence.

1. The children see the nest.

   the children see the nest

2. they see the bird

   They see the bird.

3. The bird has five eggs.

   the bird has five eggs

4. one egg falls out

   One egg falls out.

5. the boy gets the egg

   The boy gets the egg.

Home Activity Your child learned about telling sentences. Read a story together. Have your child point to sentences in the story and name the capital letter at the beginning and the period at the end.

School-Home
CONNECTION

Name _____

Telling Sentences

Which animals have you seen?

squirrel

bird

raccoon

deer

rabbit

Write about an animal you have seen.
Begin and **end** each sentence correctly.

_____

- -

_____

- -

_____

- -

_____

- -

_____

- -

_____

- -

Home Activity Your child learned how to use telling sentences when writing. Take turns with your child saying sentences that describe the animals on the page.

Telling Sentences

Find the sentence. **Mark** the sentence.

1. ○ the bird is red.
   ○ The bird is red.
   ○ the bird is red

2. ○ It has a nest.
   ○ it has a nest.
   ○ It has a nest

3. ○ the nest is brown.
   ○ the nest is brown
   ○ The nest is brown.

4. ○ An egg is in the nest.
   ○ an egg is in the nest.
   ○ An egg is in the nest

5. ○ the egg is white
   ○ the egg is white.
   ○ The egg is white.

6. ○ the bird sits on the egg.
   ○ The bird sits on the egg.
   ○ the bird sits on the egg

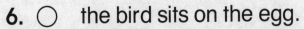

Home Activity Your child prepared for taking tests on telling sentences. Name a familiar animal. Have your child say a sentence that tells about the animal.

Telling Sentences

Put a √ by the sentence that is correct.

1. Dan sees a rabbit. _____

   dan sees a rabbit _____

2. it is in the garden _____

   It is in the garden. _____

3. The rabbit eats the plants. _____

   the rabbit eats the plants _____

Write each sentence correctly.

4. a deer is in the yard

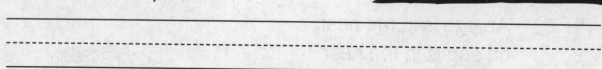

_____

- -

_____

5. it eats the bushes

_____

- -

_____

6. deer like green plants

_____

- -

_____

Home Activity Your child reviewed telling sentences. Write the three incorrect sentences from the first exercise on paper with space between them. Have your child write the sentences correctly, with a capital letter at the beginning and a period at the end.

© Pearson Education

Questions

A **question** is an asking sentence. It begins with a **capital letter**. It ends with a **question mark (?)**.

What will we see?
Is that a zebra?

Put a √ by each question.

1. Who lives in the park? _____

   Animals live in the park. _____

2. The big cats hunt. _____

   Do the big cats hunt? _____

3. Can the big birds run? _____

   The big birds can run. _____

4. Hippos like cool mud. _____

   Do hippos like cool mud? _____

5. Where are the elephants? _____

   The elephants are at the pond. _____

© Pearson Education

School-Home CONNECTION **Home Activity** Your child learned about questions. Read a story together. Have your child find any questions in the story and name the capital letter at the beginning and the punctuation mark at the end.

Questions

Finish the question. **Write** an animal name.

a zebra

a lion

a hippo

an elephant

an ostrich

_____

What does _____ look like?

Answer the question. **Write** a story.

_____
- -
_____
- -
_____
- -
_____
- -
_____

© Pearson Education

School-Home CONNECTION

Home Activity Your child learned how to use questions when writing. Say a sentence about one of the animals on the page, such as *The elephant is big*. Have your child write your sentence as a question: *Is the elephant big?*

Name _____

Questions

Find the question. **Mark** the question.

1. ○ The park big is.
   ○ is the park big?
   ○ Is the park big?

2. ○ Do animals live here?
   ○ Animals do live here.
   ○ do animals live here?

3. ○ can you see the zebras?
   ○ You can see the zebras.
   ○ Can you see the zebras?

4. ○ The big cats rest will.
   ○ Will the big cats rest?
   ○ will the big cats rest?

5. ○ are the hippos in the mud?
   ○ Are the hippos in the mud?
   ○ The hippos in the mud are.

6. ○ Do elephants swim in the pond?
   ○ do elephants swim in the pond?
   ○ Elephants do swim in the pond.

 Home Activity Your child prepared for taking tests on questions. Together listen to a conversation or an interview on TV. Each time your child hears a question, have him or her say, "Question!"

© Pearson Education

Questions

Write each question.
Begin and end the question correctly.

1. do you see a hippo

_____

- -

_____

2. is the hippo big

_____

- -

_____

3. can the hippo hide

_____

- -

_____

Look at the words. Put them in order to write a question.
Begin and end each question correctly.

4. the park what lives in

_____

- -

_____

5. the lion where is

_____

- -

_____

© Pearson Education

School-Home CONNECTION

Home Activity Your child reviewed questions. Together read a magazine article. Have your child underline any questions in the article and circle the capital letter at the beginning and the punctuation mark at the end.

Nouns

A **noun** names a person, a place, an animal, or a thing.

The word **man** names a person.   The word **park** names a place.

The word **fish** names an animal.   The word **net** names a thing.

Write the noun for each picture.

Person

girl   boy

1. _____

Place

city   pond

2. _____

Animal

cat   rabbit

3. _____

Thing

box   pan

4. _____

Home Activity Your child learned about nouns. Read a story together. Have your child point to nouns in the story and tell whether they name people, places, animals, or things.

Nouns

Write about things you do with your family.
Use words from the box or words of your own.

mom	dad	brother
grandma	grandpa	sister

_____

_____

_____

_____

_____

_____

_____

_____

_____

_____

_____

_____

_____

_____

Home Activity Your child learned how to use nouns in writing. Write sentences about family members, such as *Your sister has brown hair. Your mother loves flowers.* Have your child circle the nouns in the sentences.

© Pearson Education

Nouns

Mark the noun that completes the sentence.

1. Max wants a ___.
   - ○ eat
   - ○ fish
   - ○ will

2. The ___ has a pond.
   - ○ in
   - ○ sit
   - ○ park

3. Max got a red ___.
   - ○ ball
   - ○ talk
   - ○ this

4. A ___ is in the net.
   - ○ call
   - ○ and
   - ○ shell

5. The ___ gave them a fish.
   - ○ fat
   - ○ woman
   - ○ that

Home Activity Your child prepared for taking tests on nouns. Together read a simple piece of mail, such as an ad. Have your child circle the nouns in the article.

Grammar and Writing Practice Book   Unit 2 Week 1 **Day 4** **27**

Nouns

Circle the noun in each sentence.

1. Catch a big fish.

2. Walk to the park.

3. Dip a net.

4. See a black ship.

5. Talk to the man.

Finish each sentence.
Write a noun from the box.

| mom | grandma | dad |

_____
6. The _____ cooks eggs.

_____
7. The _____ folds things.

_____
8. The _____ feeds the baby.

Home Activity Your child reviewed nouns. Ask your child to point to and say each noun in the box. Then have your child use each noun in a sentence.

© Pearson Education

Proper Nouns

Special names for people, places, animals, and things are called **proper nouns.** Proper nouns begin with capital letters.

Meg

Rose Pond

Rex

Tell Tower

Look at each picture.
Write the proper name on the line.

Beth

1. This girl is _____.

Hall School

2. Beth goes to _____.

Post Road

3. The school is on _____.

Coco

4. The class pet is _____.

Home Activity Your child learned about proper nouns. Read a story together. Have your child point to proper nouns in the story.

© Pearson Education

Proper Nouns

Finish each sentence with a proper noun.

_____

- -

My teacher is _____.
                          (name of your teacher)

_____

- -

My school is _____.
                     (name of your school)

Write the names of three children in your class.

_____   _____   _____

- - - - - - - - - -   - - - - - - - - - -   - - - - - - - - - -

_____   _____   _____

Tell something about each child.

_____

- -

_____

- -

_____

- -

_____

- -

© Pearson Education

Home Activity Your child learned how to use proper nouns in writing. Write sentences about people that you and your child know, such as *Steve is a friend. Maria is our cousin.* Have your child circle the proper nouns in the sentences.

Name _____

Proper Nouns

Mark the sentence that uses the proper noun correctly.

1. ○ This boy is jake.
   ○ This boy is Jake.
   ○ This boy is JAKE.

2. ○ He has a dog named PIP.
   ○ He has a dog named pip.
   ○ He has a dog named Pip.

3. ○ This girl is Grace.
   ○ This girl is GRACE.
   ○ This girl is grace.

4. ○ She has a cat named KIT.
   ○ She has a cat named kit.
   ○ She has a cat named Kit.

5. ○ The children go to Tam School.
   ○ The children go to tam School.
   ○ The children go to Tam school.

6. ○ The school is on elm Street.
   ○ The school is on Elm Street.
   ○ The school is on Elm street.

Home Activity Your child prepared for taking tests on proper nouns. Together read a short newspaper or magazine article. Have your child circle the proper nouns in the article.

School-Home CONNECTION

© Pearson Education

Proper Nouns

Circle the proper noun in each pair.

1. boy   Dave

2. Zippy   cat

3. Beth   girl

4. town   Alton

Write the sentences.
Use a capital letter for each proper noun.

1. We are at beck zoo.

_____

- -

_____

2. The zoo is on king road.

_____

- -

_____

3. The lion is named sam.

_____

- -

_____

4. Does meg see the lion?

_____

- -

_____

Home Activity Your child reviewed proper nouns. Ask your child to point to and say each proper noun on the page. Then have your child use each proper noun in a sentence.

Special Titles

A **title** can come before the name of a person. A title begins with a capital letter. Some titles end with a **period (.)**.

Doctor Silva   **Mrs.** Faber   **Mr.** Gray

Write the title and the name correctly on the line.

1. miss oda

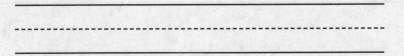

2. captain bartz

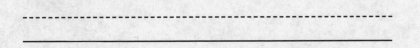

3. dr. hashmi

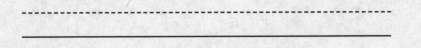

4. ms. ford

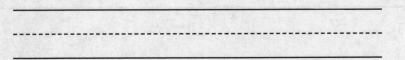

Home Activity Your child learned about special titles. Say the names and titles of adults your child knows, for example, *Dr. Kahn, Ms. Bell, Mr. Garcia.* Ask your child to identify and write the person's title.

School-Home CONNECTION

© Pearson Education

Special Titles

Tell about people who work in your community.
Use words from the box or your own words.
Use titles and names.

teacher	mail carrier	police officer
doctor	vet	librarian

_____

- -

_____

_____

- -

_____

_____

- -

_____

_____

- -

_____

Home Activity Your child learned how to use special titles in writing. Write these titles and names on paper: *mr jones, ms gold, dr novak*. Have your child explain what is wrong and write the titles and names correctly.

Grammar and Writing Practice Book

Special Titles

Mark the sentence that uses the title and name correctly.

1. ○ Our doctor is Dr. Brown.
   ○ Our doctor is Dr. brown.
   ○ Our doctor is dr. Brown.

2. ○ My teacher is ms. Okada.
   ○ My teacher is Ms. Okada.
   ○ My teacher is Ms okada.

3. ○ Mr diaz brings our mail.
   ○ mr. Diaz brings our mail.
   ○ Mr. Diaz brings our mail.

4. ○ Our vet is Doctor tang.
   ○ Our vet is doctor Tang.
   ○ Our vet is Doctor Tang.

5. ○ miss Vale works at the library.
   ○ Miss Vale works at the library.
   ○ Miss vale works at the library.

6. ○ Mrs. Benik drives our bus.
   ○ Mrs. benik drives our bus.
   ○ mrs. Benik drives our bus.

Home Activity Your child prepared for taking tests on special titles. Together look through a newspaper or magazine. Have your child find and circle as many special titles as he or she can.

© Pearson Education

Special Titles

Write the title and the name correctly on the line.

I. ms. choi

_____

- -

_____

2. mr. jung

_____

- -

_____

3. dr. ortiz

_____

- -

_____

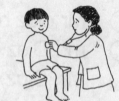

Write each sentence correctly.
Use capital letters for the titles and names.

4. The teacher is mr rabin.

_____

- -

_____

5. Our dentist is dr bondi.

_____

- -

_____

6. Do you know miss barton?

_____

- -

_____

Home Activity Your child reviewed special titles. Ask your child to point to each title and name on the page and explain what he or she did to correct each.

Grammar and Writing Practice Book

Days, Months, and Holidays

Days of the week begin with capital letters.

Sunday   Wednesday   Saturday

Months of the year begin with capital letters.

February   May   October

Holidays begin with capital letters.

Fourth of July   Memorial Day

Write the day, month, or holiday correctly on the line.

1. We learn about dinosaurs on monday.

   _____
   -
   _____

2. On thursday a man tells us about dinosaurs.

   _____
   -
   _____

3. In november we put on a play about dinosaurs.

   _____
   -
   _____

4. The play tells about dinosaurs at thanksgiving!

   _____
   -
   _____

© Pearson Education

School-Home CONNECTION

Home Activity Your child learned about days, months, and holidays. Say the names of a day, a month, and a holiday and help your child write each name. Be sure each name begins with a capital letter.

Name _____

Days, Months, and Holidays

Tell about a picnic, a fair, or a party.
Use the name of a month or holiday.

February	October	Valentine's Day
May	November	Fourth of July
July	December	Thanksgiving

_____
- - - - - - - - - - - - - - - - - -
_____

_____
- - - - - - - - - - - - - - - - - -
_____

_____
- - - - - - - - - - - - - - - - - -
_____

_____
- - - - - - - - - - - - - - - - - -
_____

Home Activity Your child learned how to use days, months, and holidays in writing. Write these names on paper: *tuesday, april, halloween*. Have your child explain what is wrong and write the names correctly.

Days, Months, and Holidays

Mark the sentence that uses the day, month, or holiday correctly.

1. ○ On Tuesday we collect cans.
   ○ On tuesday we collect cans.
   ○ On TuesDay we collect cans.

2. ○ A truck picks up the cans on friday.
   ○ A truck picks up the cans on Friday.
   ○ A truck picks up the cans on FRiday.

3. ○ The neighbors plant a garden in june.
   ○ The neighbors plant a garden in JUne.
   ○ The neighbors plant a garden in June.

4. ○ In august they pick the vegetables.
   ○ In August they pick the vegetables.
   ○ In AuGust they pick the vegetables.

5. ○ On memorial Day our town has a parade.
   ○ On Memorial day our town has a parade.
   ○ On Memorial Day our town has a parade.

6. ○ We watch fireworks on the Fourth of July.
   ○ We watch fireworks on the fourth of July.
   ○ We watch fireworks on the Fourth of july.

Home Activity Your child prepared for taking tests on days, months, and holidays. Together look through a newspaper or magazine. Have your child find and circle any days, months, and holidays that he or she finds.

Days, Months, and Holidays

Write the day, month, or holiday correctly on the line.

1. Our town has a fair in september.

    _____

    _____

2. The fair begins on labor day.

    _____

    _____

3. We went to the fair on friday.

    _____

    _____

Finish the sentences.
Write a day, a month, or a holiday.

    _____

    ----

4. Today is _____.

    _____

    ----

5. This month is _____.

    _____

    ----

6. The best holiday is _____.

Home Activity Your child reviewed days, months, and holidays. Talk with your child about things your family does during the week or the year. Each time you mention a day, month, or holiday, have your child write the name.

One and More Than One

Many nouns add **-s** to mean more than one.

tree

tree**s**

Draw a line from the noun to the correct picture.

I. bug bugs	**2.** rocks rock
3. plants plant	**4.** log logs

School-Home CONNECTION

Home Activity Your child learned about plural nouns. Write the words *desk, lamp, chair, table,* and *cup.* Have your child add *-s* to each word to make it mean more than one.

© Pearson Education

Name _____

One and More Than One

Pretend you are in this park.
Tell about the plants and animals you see.

trees   flowers   squirrels   birds   rabbits

_____

- -

_____

- -

_____

- -

_____

- -

_____

- -

_____

© Pearson Education

Home Activity Your child learned how to use plural nouns in writing. Read a story together. Ask your child to point out any words he or she sees that mean more than one.

42 Unit 2 Week 5 **Day 3**   **Grammar and Writing Practice Book**

One and More Than One

Mark the word that shows more than one.

I. Look at the two frogs.
- ○ the
- ○ Look
- ○ frogs

2. The bird eats the bugs.
- ○ bugs
- ○ eat
- ○ bird

3. The tree has three holes.
- ○ has
- ○ holes
- ○ tree

4. A bear is by the rocks.
- ○ bear
- ○ rocks
- ○ by

5. The squirrel hides the nuts.
- ○ nuts
- ○ squirrel
- ○ The

Home Activity Your child prepared for taking tests on plural nouns. Together look through a newspaper or magazine. Have your child find and circle as many plural nouns as he or she can.

One and More Than One

Finish the sentences.
Write the correct word on the line.

1. Three _____ are by the tree.
   (rocks, rocks)

2. Six _____ are on the rocks.
   (bug, bugs)

3. One _____ eats the bugs.
   (frog, frogs)

4. Two _____ sit on a log.
   (bird, birds)

5. One _____ eats the nuts.
   (bear, bears)

6. Three _____ have flowers.
   (plant, plants)

School-Home CONNECTION

Home Activity Your child reviewed plural nouns. Point to objects around your home and help your child write the name of the object and its plural form.

Name _____

Nouns in Sentences

A **noun** names a person, a place, an animal, or a thing. A noun can be in more than one place in a sentence.

Bees live in a **hive**.

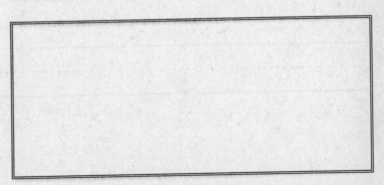

_____

Circle the noun in each sentence.
Draw and **color** a picture for each noun.

1. The sun is warm.

2. Look at the bee.

3. Where is the flower?

Home Activity Your child learned about nouns in sentences. Read a story together. Point to a sentence and have your child point to the nouns in the sentence. Continue with other sentences.

© Pearson Education

Nouns in Sentences

Bees are like a family.
Bees have special jobs.
Do people in your family have special jobs?
Write about the jobs.

_____

- -

_____

_____

- -

_____

_____

- -

_____

_____

- -

_____

_____

- -

_____

School-Home CONNECTION

Home Activity Your child learned how to use nouns when writing sentences. Take turns with your child telling about jobs that you do at home. Have your child identify any nouns either of you uses in your sentences.

Grammar and Writing Practice Book

Name _____

Nouns in Sentences

Mark the sentence that has a line under the noun.

1. ○ The bees <u>wake</u> up.
   ○ The <u>bees</u> wake up.
   ○ The bees wake <u>up</u>.

2. ○ Look <u>at</u> the hive.
   ○ Look at the hive.
   ○ Look at the <u>hive</u>.

3. ○ Jan likes sweet <u>honey</u>.
   ○ Jan likes <u>sweet</u> honey.
   ○ Jan <u>likes</u> sweet honey.

4. ○ The workers <u>get</u> mad.
   ○ The workers get <u>mad</u>.
   ○ The <u>workers</u> get mad.

5. ○ Where does <u>pollen</u> come from?
   ○ Where <u>does</u> pollen come from?
   ○ Where does pollen <u>come</u> from?

6. ○ A family <u>lives</u> together.
   ○ A <u>family</u> lives together.
   ○ A family lives <u>together</u>.

 Home Activity Your child prepared for taking tests on nouns in sentences. Together read a simple newspaper or magazine article. Have your child circle as many nouns as he or she can find.

Grammar and Writing Practice Book Unit 2 Week 6 **Day 4** 47

Name _____

Nouns in Sentences

Circle the two nouns in each sentence.

1. The sun wakes up the bees.

2. Every hive has a queen.

3. Workers find sweet nectar.

4. Cells are small holes.

5. A big bear wants the honey.

Finish the sentences.
Write a noun from the box.

6. _____ are insects.

7. Bees live in a _____.

8. The bees see _____.

Home Activity Your child reviewed nouns in sentences. Write this sentence frame on paper: *A ___ has ___.* Take turns with your child completing the sentence with two nouns, for example, *A cat has fur. A dog has legs. A bee has wings.*

Grammar and Writing Practice Book

Action Verbs

A **verb** tells what someone or something does.

The baby **crawls.**

The boy **walks.**

Underline the verb in each sentence.

1. A tree grows green leaves.

2. The leaves fall to the ground.

3. The wind blows the leaves.

4. A hen lays an egg.

5. The hen sits on the egg.

6. A chick hatches from the egg.

Home Activity Your child learned about verbs. Read a story together. Point to a sentence and have your child point to the verb in the sentence. Continue with other sentences.

© Pearson Education

Action Verbs

Write about things you do every day.
Use action verbs from the box or your own words.

eat	go	read
sleep	play	talk

_____

- -

_____

_____

- -

_____

_____

- -

_____

_____

- -

_____

_____

- -

_____

Home Activity Your child learned how to use verbs in writing. Take turns with your child telling about things that you do every day. Have your child identify any action verbs either of you uses in your sentences.

Action Verbs

Mark the sentence that has a line under the verb.

1. ○ Ann <u>plants</u> a seed.
   ○ Ann plants a seed.
   ○ Ann plants a <u>seed</u>.

2. ○ She pushes it into <u>the</u> ground.
   ○ She pushes <u>it</u> into the ground.
   ○ She <u>pushes</u> it into the ground.

3. ○ Rain <u>falls</u> on the ground.
   ○ <u>Rain</u> falls on the ground.
   ○ Rain falls on the <u>ground</u>.

4. ○ The sun shines on <u>the</u> ground.
   ○ The sun shines <u>on</u> the ground.
   ○ The sun <u>shines</u> on the ground.

5. ○ The seed <u>grows</u> into a plant.
   ○ The seed <u>grows</u> into a plant.
   ○ The seed grows into a <u>plant</u>.

6. ○ <u>A</u> flower blooms on the plant.
   ○ A flower <u>blooms</u> on the plant.
   ○ A flower blooms <u>on</u> the plant.

Home Activity Your child prepared for taking tests on verbs. Together read a short, simple newspaper or magazine article. Have your child circle as many action verbs as he or she can find.

© Pearson Education

Action Verbs

Circle the verb in each sentence.

1. The baby cries in its crib.

2. The puppy runs to its mother.

3. The kitten plays with a string.

Circle the correct verb in ( ) to complete each sentence.
Write the verb on the line.

4. The boy _____ to his friend.

(bakes, calls)

5. The dog _____ at the man.

(barks, talks)

6. The cat _____ a fish.

(sings, eats)

School-Home CONNECTION

Home Activity Your child reviewed verbs. Write this sentence frame on paper: *The child ____.* Take turns with your child completing the sentence with an action verb, for example, *The child runs. The child walks. The child laughs.*

Grammar and Writing Practice Book

Name _____

Verbs That Add -s

A **verb** can tell what one person, animal, or thing does. Add **-s** to show what is being done now.

Ruby **grows** bigger.   Ruby **spreads** her wings.

Complete each sentence.
Write the correct word on the line.

1. Pam _____ a book.
   (reads, read)

2. Ned _____ a cake.
   (bake, bakes)

3. José _____ a bike.
   (rides, ride)

4. Tina _____ her shoes.
   (tie, ties)

Home Activity Your child learned about verbs that add -s. Write the words *swim, run, walk, jump,* and *dance* on paper. Have your child add an -s to each word and then act out the word.

© Pearson Education

Verbs That Add -s

Look at the picture.
Write a verb to finish each sentence.
Remember to add -s to each verb.
Add more words to the sentence if you want.

The girl _____

_____

The boy _____

_____

The dad _____

_____

The mom _____

_____

The dog _____

© Pearson Education

School-Home CONNECTION

Home Activity Your child learned how to use verbs that add -s in writing. Write these sentence frames on paper: *Dan* _____. *Anna* _____. Have your child write verbs that add -s to each sentence frame to make as many sentences as possible.

Name _____

Verbs That Add -s

Mark the sentence that is correct.

1. ○ Amy plays a song.
   ○ Amys plays a song.
   ○ Amy plays a songs.

2. ○ Johns writes his name.
   ○ John writes his name.
   ○ John writes hiss name.

3. ○ Rosa makes one big pizzas.
   ○ Rosa makes one bigs pizza.
   ○ Rosa makes one big pizza.

4. ○ Daves runs a long race.
   ○ Dave runs a long race.
   ○ Dave runs a longs race.

5. ○ Kate learns a new game.
   ○ Kates learns a new game.
   ○ Kate learns a new games.

6. ○ Sam spells a hards word.
   ○ Sam spells a hard words.
   ○ Sam spells a hard word.

Home Activity Your child prepared for taking tests on verbs that add -s. Together read a short, simple newspaper or magazine article. Have your child find and circle as many verbs that end in -s as possible.

Grammar and Writing Practice Book

© Pearson Education

Verbs That Add -s

Complete each sentence. **Underline** the correct verb.

1. The baby (needs, need) milk.

2. The boy (walk, walks) to school.

3. The man (works, work) at a store.

Add -s to the verb in ( ) to complete each sentence.
Write the verb on the line.

4. The puppy _____ in the box. (sleep)

5. The dog _____ through a hoop. (jump)

6. Spot _____ up the paper. (pick)

School-Home CONNECTION

Home Activity Your child reviewed verbs that add -s. Have your child point to each verb on this page that ends in -s and use the word in a new sentence.

© Pearson Education

Verbs That Do Not Add -s

Do not add **-s** to a verb that tells what two or more people, animals, or things do now.

Meg and Jen **move** to a new house.

Circle the verb that shows more than one.

1. Meg and Jen (pack, packs) the toys.

2. The toys (fills, fill) ten boxes.

3. Two men (load, loads) the truck.

Circle the correct verb. **Write** the verb on the line.

4. The girls _____ many flowers.
   (see, sees)

5. Horses _____ on the grass.
   (runs, run)

School-Home CONNECTION

Home Activity Your child learned about verbs that do not add -s. Write this sentence beginning: *The children ___.* Then act out a verb, such as *swim, run, walk, jump,* and *dance.* Have your child say the verb to finish the sentence.

Name _____

Verbs That Do Not Add *-s*

Pretend you see two new girls at school.
Write about what you do.
Write about what they do.
Begin your sentences with <u>we</u> and <u>they</u>.

_____

- - - - - - - - - - - - - - - - - - -

_____

- - - - - - - - - - - - - - - - - - -

_____

- - - - - - - - - - - - - - - - - - -

_____

- - - - - - - - - - - - - - - - - - -

_____

- - - - - - - - - - - - - - - - - - -

_____

- - - - - - - - - - - - - - - - - - -

_____

© Pearson Education

School-Home CONNECTION

Home Activity Your child learned how to use verbs that do not add *-s* in writing. Point to pictures that show more than one person, animal, or thing. Ask: *What do the (children, birds, etc.) do?* Have your child write the answer to the question.

Verbs That Do Not Add -s

Mark the sentence that is correct.

1. ○ Ann and Pat walks to a new school.
   ○ Ann walk to a new school.
   ○ Ann and Pat walk to a new school.

2. ○ The girls like their old school.
   ○ The girls likes their old school.
   ○ The girl like their old school.

3. ○ Their friend live in another town.
   ○ Their friends live in another town.
   ○ Their friends lives in another town.

4. ○ Ben and Vic talk to the girls.
   ○ Ben talk to the girls.
   ○ Ben and Vic talks to the girls.

5. ○ The boy tell about the new school.
   ○ The boys tell about the new school.
   ○ The boys tells about the new school.

6. ○ Pat feel better.
   ○ Ann and Pat feels better.
   ○ Ann and Pat feel better.

Home Activity Your child prepared for taking tests on verbs that do not add -s. Together read a paragraph from a newspaper or magazine article. Have your child find and circle verbs that do not end in -s.

Grammar and Writing Practice Book

Name _____

Verbs That Do Not Add -s

Circle the verb that shows more than one.

1. Jan and her parents (moves, move) to the city.

2. Her parents (drive, drives) the car.

3. They (sees, see) horses and sheep.

Circle the correct verb. **Write** the verb on the line.

4. Cars _____ the road.
(fills, fill)

5. Trucks _____ by.
(roar, roars)

6. The men _____ at Jan.
(waves, wave)

School-Home CONNECTION

Home Activity Your child reviewed verbs that do not add -s. Have your child point to each verb on this page that does not end in -s and use the word in a new sentence.

Grammar and Writing Practice Book

Verbs for Now and the Past

Verbs can tell what happens now. Verbs can tell what happened in the past. Some verbs that tell about the past end with **-ed**.

Toad **walks**. (now)   Toad **walked**. (past)

Read each word in the box. **Write** the word under *Now* if it tells about now. **Write** the word under *The Past* if it tells about the past.

wants	liked	jumped
helped	shouts	asks

Now   ### The Past

1. _____

2. _____

3. _____

4. _____

5. _____

6. _____

Home Activity Your child learned about verbs for now and the past. Write the verbs *talk, laugh,* and *yell* on paper. Have your child add *-s* and *-ed* to each word and tell whether each new word tells about now or the past.

School-Home CONNECTION

Verbs for Now and the Past

In the past you were a baby.
Tell about things you did then.

_____

- -

_____

- -

_____

- -

_____

Now you are in first grade.
Tell about things you do now.

_____

- -

_____

- -

_____

- -

_____

Home Activity Your child learned how to use verbs for now and the past in writing. With your child, look through a family photo album. Talk about what you were doing then using verbs for the past. Talk about what you are doing now using verbs for now.

© Pearson Education

Verbs for Now and the Past

Mark the sentence that is correct.

1. ○ Last year Joe tends a garden.
   ○ Last year Joe tend a garden.
   ○ Last year Joe tended a garden.

2. ○ Now Jan wants a garden.
   ○ Now Jan wanted a garden.
   ○ Now Jan want a garden.

3. ○ Last week Beth works in the garden.
   ○ Last week Beth worked in the garden.
   ○ Last week Beth work in the garden.

4. ○ Today Sam helps Beth.
   ○ Today Sam helped Beth.
   ○ Today Sam help Beth.

5. ○ Last month Ali pick red roses.
   ○ Last month Ali picked red roses.
   ○ Last month Ali picks red roses.

6. ○ Now Dan looked for white tulips.
   ○ Now Dan look for white tulips.
   ○ Now Dan looks for white tulips.

Home Activity Your child prepared for taking tests on verbs for now and the past. Together read part of a newspaper or magazine article. Have your child circle verbs that tell about now and underline verbs that tell about the past.

Grammar and Writing Practice Book   Unit 3 Week 4 **Day 4** **63**

© Pearson Education

Name _____

Verbs for Now and the Past

Circle the correct verb in ( ).

1. Last month Frog (started, starts) a garden.

2. Now Toad (started, starts) a garden.

3. Last month Frog (planted, plants) seeds.

4. Now Toad (planted, plants) seeds.

Complete each sentence. **Write** the correct verb on the line.

5. Yesterday Toad _____ at the seeds.
(looks, looked)

6. Last night he _____ at them.
(shouts, shouted)

7. Today Toad _____ music for them.
(plays, played)

8. Now he _____ for the flowers.
(waits, waited)

Home Activity Your child reviewed verbs for now and the past. Write *Now* and *The Past* on paper. Ask your child to write all the verbs in items 1-8 on this page under the correct heading.

Grammar and Writing Practice Book

Am, Is, Are, Was, and Were

The words **am, is,** and **are** tell about now. Use **am** or **is** to tell about one. Use **are** to tell about more than one.

I **am** big.   It **is** little.   They **are** tiny.

The words **was** and **were** tell about the past. Use **was** to tell about one. Use **were** to tell about more than one.

It **was** hungry.   They **were** hungry.

Circle the verb in each sentence. **Write** *Now* if the sentence tells about now. **Write** *Past* if the sentence tells about the past.

1. I was an egg.   _____

2. I am a caterpillar.   _____

3. They are caterpillars.   _____

4. They were eggs.   _____

5. The change is amazing.   _____

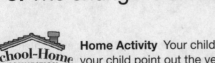

Home Activity Your child learned about *am, is, are, was,* and *were.* Read a story with your child. Have your child point out the verbs *am, is, are, was,* and *were* in the story and tell whether the sentence tells about now or the past.

Name _____

Am, Is, Are, Was, and Were

Look at the picture.
Tell about what you see.
Use *am*, *is*, *are*, *was*, or *were*.

_____

- -

_____

- -

_____

- -

_____

- -

_____

- -

_____

- -

Home Activity Your child learned how to use *am, is, are, was,* and *were* in writing. Write these sentence frames on paper: *Today I ___ happy. Now he ___ happy. Yesterday she ___ happy. Now they ___ happy. Yesterday we ___ happy.* Have your child complete the sentences with *am, is, are, was,* and *were.*

Grammar and Writing Practice Book

Am, Is, Are, Was, and Were

Mark the sentence that is correct.

1. ○ Raj is in the garden.
   ○ Raj am in the garden.
   ○ Raj are in the garden.

2. ○ Butterflies is on the flowers.
   ○ Butterflies was on the flowers.
   ○ Butterflies are on the flowers.

3. ○ One butterfly were yellow.
   ○ One butterfly was yellow.
   ○ One butterfly are yellow.

4. ○ Those flowers am white.
   ○ Those flowers was white.
   ○ Those flowers were white.

5. ○ I am next to Raj.
   ○ I are next to Raj.
   ○ I is next to Raj.

6. ○ We am happy in the garden.
   ○ We are happy in the garden.
   ○ We was happy in the garden.

Home Activity Your child prepared for taking tests on *am, is, are, was,* and *were*. Together read part of a newspaper or magazine article. Have your child circle the verbs *am, is, are, was,* and *were*.

School-Home CONNECTION

© Pearson Education

Name _____

Am, Is, Are, Was, and Were

Circle the verb in ( ) that completes each sentence correctly.

1. Today I (am, is) in the yard.

2. A caterpillar (are, is) on my arm.

3. A butterfly (was, were) on my hand.

4. Last week the butterflies (were, was) red.

5. Today the butterflies (is, are) white.

Choose the correct verb in ( ) to complete the sentence.
Write the verb on the line.

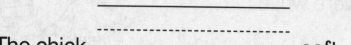

6. Eggs _____ small.
   (are, is)

7. The chick _____ soft.
   (am, is)

8. The hen _____ hungry.
   (was, were)

School-Home CONNECTION

Home Activity Your child reviewed *am, is, are, was,* and *were.* Write *am, is, are, was,* and *were* on paper. With your child, take turns pointing to a verb and using it in a sentence.

Grammar and Writing Practice Book

© Pearson Education

Contractions with *Not*

A **contraction** is a short way to put two words together. A **verb** and the word **not** can be put together to make a contraction. An **apostrophe** (') is used in place of the letter **o** in **not**.

are + not = aren't   has + not = hasn't
did + not = didn't   is + not = isn't
do + not = don't   was + not = wasn't
does + not = doesn't   were + not = weren't

Circle the contraction in each sentence.

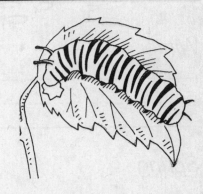

1. The animals don't have much time.

2. Caterpillar doesn't come out until spring.

3. Goose isn't staying for the winter.

Write the contraction for the underlined words.

4. The leaves <u>are not</u> on the trees.   _____

5. Raccoon <u>was not</u> leaving the forest.   _____

Home Activity Your child learned about contractions with *not*. Read a story with your child. Have your child look for contractions with *not* and tell the two words that were put together to make each contraction.

Contractions with *Not*

Write a sentence about each season.
Use a contraction with *not* in each sentence.

Winter

_____

- -

_____

Spring

_____

- -

_____

Summer

_____

- -

_____

Fall

_____

- -

_____

Home Activity Your child learned how to use contractions with *not* in writing. Write these sentences on paper: *He does not like winter. They do not like summer. She is not sad in the fall. We are not cold in the spring.* Have your child write the sentences using contractions with *not*.

© Pearson Education

Contractions with *Not*

Mark the sentence that spells the contraction correctly.

1. ○ Days aren't long in the winter.
   ○ Days arent long in the winter.
   ○ Days are'nt long in the winter.

2. ○ A raccoon does'nt sleep all winter long.
   ○ A raccoon doesnt sleep all winter long.
   ○ A raccoon doesn't sleep all winter long.

3. ○ The chrysalis hasnt moved at all.
   ○ The chrysalis hasn't moved at all.
   ○ The chrysalis has'nt moved at all.

4. ○ Bears do'nt come out until spring.
   ○ Bears dont come out until spring.
   ○ Bears don't come out until spring.

5. ○ Many birds didn't stay here.
   ○ Many birds did'nt stay here.
   ○ Many birds didnt stay here.

6. ○ The fat bear was'nt hungry.
   ○ The fat bear wasn't hungry.
   ○ The fat bear wasnt hungry.

Home Activity Your child prepared for taking tests on contractions with *not*. Together read part of a short newspaper or magazine article. Take turns with your child circling contractions with *not*. Ask your child what two words make up each contraction.

Contractions with *Not*

Draw a line from the words to their contraction.

1. are not   doesn't
2. did not   wasn't
3. do not   hasn't
4. does not   aren't
5. has not   weren't
6. is not   didn't
7. was not   don't
8. were not   isn't

Write the contraction for the underlined words.

9. A bear <u>does not</u> eat all winter. _____

10. Bears <u>do not</u> wake up until spring. _____

11. Squirrels <u>are not</u> going away. _____

12. The squirrel <u>was not</u> in its nest. _____

Home Activity Your child reviewed contractions with *not*. Have your child write contractions with *not* on one side of index cards and the words for each contraction on the other side. Use the flash cards to test your child.

Adjectives

An **adjective** tells about a person, place, animal, or thing.

happy woman   **big** city   **loud** dog   **nice** present

Circle the adjective. **Write** the adjective on the line.

1. heavy piñata   _____

2. bright lights   _____

3. hot tortillas   _____

4. good friends   _____

5. sweet rolls   _____

Home Activity Your child learned about adjectives. Read a story with your child. Point to a sentence and ask your child to identify any adjectives in the sentence. Continue with other sentences.

© Pearson Education

Name _____

Adjectives

Write an adjective from the box to complete each sentence.

| green | sharp | soft |

1. Gina's cat has _____ fur.

2. The cat has _____ eyes.

3. Look at the cat's _____ claws.

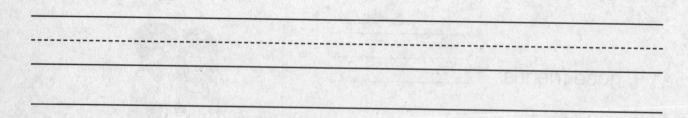

Tell about something you like.
Use adjectives to describe it.

_____

_____

_____

_____

_____

Home Activity Your child learned how to use adjectives in writing. Take turns with your child describing what you are wearing. Have your child identify any adjectives either of you uses in your descriptions.

Grammar and Writing Practice Book

© Pearson Education

Adjectives

Mark the sentence that has a line under the adjective.

1. ○ Grandmother reads a <u>funny</u> book.
   ○ Grandmother <u>reads</u> a funny book.
   ○ <u>Grandmother</u> reads a funny book.

2. ○ Mama <u>gave</u> Francisco a big hug.
   ○ Mama gave Francisco a <u>big</u> hug.
   ○ Mama gave Francisco a big <u>hug</u>.

3. ○ Francisco <u>made</u> a colorful piñata.
   ○ <u>Francisco</u> made a colorful piñata.
   ○ Francisco made a <u>colorful</u> piñata.

4. ○ Everyone <u>ate</u> the fresh tortillas.
   ○ Everyone ate the fresh <u>tortillas</u>.
   ○ Everyone ate the <u>fresh</u> tortillas.

5. ○ The <u>party</u> was the best present.
   ○ The party was the <u>best</u> present.
   ○ The party was the best <u>present</u>.

6. ○ Papa played a <u>long</u> song.
   ○ Papa <u>played</u> a long song.
   ○ <u>Papa</u> played a long song.

School-Home CONNECTION

Home Activity Your child prepared for taking tests on adjectives. Together read a short, simple newspaper or magazine article. Have your child circle as many adjectives as he or she can find.

Adjectives

Look at the pictures.
Complete each sentence.
Underline the correct adjective.

1. This is a (happy, sad) boy.

2. He has a (rusty, new) bike.

3. The bike has (black, white) wheels.

Complete each sentence.
Write an adjective from the box.

funny	soft	little

4. Joe has a _____ car.

5. Babies like _____ toys.

6. Nan loves _____ hats.

Home Activity Your child reviewed adjectives. Take turns with your child replacing the adjectives in these phrases: *funny hat, little animal, happy child.* (Examples: *warm hat, red hat; big animal, wild animal; sad child, angry child*)

Grammar and Writing Practice Book

Adjectives for Colors and Shapes

Some **adjectives** name colors.

white crayon   **black** pencil

Some **adjectives** name shapes.

square paper   **round** frame

Circle the adjective in each sentence that names a color or shape.

1. Karl has blue markers.

2. Ali has green markers.

3. Karl draws round circles.

4. Ali draws square boxes.

5. Karl adds brown dots.

6. Ali makes yellow lines.

School-Home CONNECTION **Home Activity** Your child learned about adjectives for colors and shapes. Point to objects around your home and have your child describe the objects using adjectives that name colors and shapes.

Name _____

Adjectives for Colors and Shapes

Color the boxes and circles.

Write about the picture.
Use color and shape words.

_____

_____

_____

_____

_____

_____

_____

_____

_____

_____

Home Activity Your child learned how to use adjectives for colors and shapes in writing. Write this sentence frame on paper: *The ___ animal runs.* Have your child write color adjectives in the sentence frame to make as many sentences as possible.

© Pearson Education

Adjectives for Colors and Shapes

Mark the sentence that has a line under the adjective.

1. ○ Will Cam draw yellow flowers?
   ○ Will Cam draw yellow flowers?
   ○ Will Cam draw yellow flowers?

2. ○ She makes round shapes.
   ○ She makes round shapes.
   ○ She makes round shapes.

3. ○ She adds green stems.
   ○ She adds green stems.
   ○ She adds green stems.

4. ○ Ty cuts brown paper.
   ○ Ty cuts brown paper.
   ○ Ty cuts brown paper.

5. ○ He pastes it on square boxes.
   ○ He pastes it on square boxes.
   ○ He pastes it on square boxes.

6. ○ He makes lines with black markers.
   ○ He makes lines with black markers.
   ○ He makes lines with black markers.

© Pearson Education

Home Activity Your child prepared for taking tests on adjectives for colors and shapes. Together read a favorite book. Have your child point out adjectives that name colors and shapes.

Name _____

Adjectives for Colors and Shapes

Underline the adjective to make each sentence correct.

1. Sue has a pile of (red, get) beads.

2. She puts them on (smile, white) string.

3. Jeff takes some (green, sleep) clay.

4. He bends it into (stand, round) shapes.

Choose the adjective in ( ).
Write the adjective on the line.

5. Mom cuts _____ pieces of cloth.
   (square, shout)

6. I add _____ buttons.
   (blow, blue)

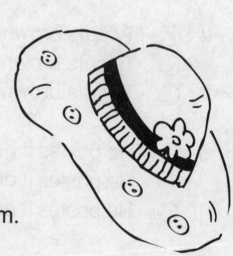

7. Mom sews on _____ trim.
   (black, talk)

8. I love my _____ hat!
   (think, pink)

 School-Home CONNECTION

Home Activity Your child reviewed adjectives for colors and shapes. Have your child point to each adjective on this page that names a color or shape and use the word in a new sentence.

© Pearson Education

Name _____

Adjectives for Sizes

Some **adjectives** describe size. Words such as **big, small, long,** and **short** describe size.

small animal

big animal

Circle each adjective that describes size.

I. big kite

2. long tail

3. little rabbit

4. short tail

5. tall plant

6. huge head

School-Home
CONNECTION

Home Activity Your child learned about adjectives for sizes. Point to objects around your home. Ask your child if the object is big or small (tall or short, long or short). Have your child answer using the adjective in a sentence.

Adjectives for Sizes

Write about something you like that is very big.
It might be an animal, a place, or a thing.
Use adjectives to tell about it.

_____

- -

_____

_____

- -

_____

_____

- -

_____

Write about something you like that is very small.
It might be an animal, a place, or a thing.
Use adjectives to tell about it.

_____

- -

_____

_____

- -

_____

_____

- -

_____

© Pearson Education

School-Home CONNECTION

Home Activity Your child learned how to use adjectives for sizes in writing. Point to pictures that show big, small, long, short, and tall things, one at a time. Ask: *What size is the ___?* Have your child answer the question.

Grammar and Writing Practice Book

Adjectives for Sizes

Mark the sentence that has a line under the adjective.

1. ○ Mr. Brown <u>found</u> big bones.
   ○ Mr. Brown found <u>big</u> bones.
   ○ Mr. Brown found <u>big</u> bones.

2. ○ The dinosaur had <u>short</u> arms.
   ○ The dinosaur had <u>short</u> arms.
   ○ The dinosaur had short <u>arms</u>.

3. ○ T. rex <u>was</u> a tall dinosaur.
   ○ T. rex was a <u>tall</u> dinosaur.
   ○ T. rex was a <u>tall</u> dinosaur.

4. ○ Ms. Gupta found <u>small</u> pots.
   ○ Ms. Gupta found <u>small</u> pots.
   ○ Ms. Gupta found small <u>pots</u>.

5. ○ This <u>pot</u> has a little handle.
   ○ This pot has a <u>little</u> handle.
   ○ This pot has a little <u>handle</u>.

6. ○ That pot <u>has</u> a long neck.
   ○ That pot has a long <u>neck</u>.
   ○ That pot has a <u>long</u> neck.

Home Activity Your child prepared for taking tests on adjectives for sizes. Together read a favorite storybook. Have your child find adjectives for sizes.

© Pearson Education

Adjectives for Sizes

Circle the adjective that describes size.

1. short pony

2. small baby

3. big chair

Look at the pictures. **Write** the adjective in ( ) that tells about each picture.

4. _____ dinosaur
(huge, tiny)

5. _____ pet
(little, big)

6. _____ dress
(short, long)

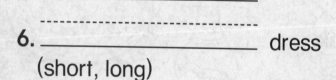

Home Activity Your child reviewed adjectives for sizes. Have your child point to each adjective on this page and use the word in a new sentence.

Grammar and Writing Practice Book

Adjectives for What Kind

An **adjective** can tell what kind.

sweet cherries

ripe pears

Write the adjective that tells what kind.

1. juicy watermelon

_____

2. firm plums

_____

3. hot rice

_____

4. bright lantern

_____

5. smooth paper

_____

6. dark night

_____

School-Home CONNECTION

Home Activity Your child learned about adjectives for what kind. Write *hot, cold, dry* in one list and the nouns *snow, sun, socks* in another list. Ask your child to combine the adjectives and nouns (*hot sun, cold snow, dry socks*).

© Pearson Education

Name _____

Adjectives for What Kind

Write about something your family does
every Fourth of July or another holiday.
Use adjectives such as *loud*, *tasty*,
or *cold* to tell about it.

_____

- -

_____

- -

_____

- -

_____

- -

_____

- -

_____

- -

_____

- -

_____

- -

_____

- -

_____

- -

_____

Home Activity Your child learned how to use adjectives for what kind in writing. With your child, look through a family photo album. Talk about what you see in photos using adjectives that tell what kind.

Grammar and Writing Practice Book

Adjectives for What Kind

Mark the sentence that has a line under the adjective.

1. ○ <u>Dinner</u> on Sunday is a great meal.
   ○ Dinner on <u>Sunday</u> is a great meal.
   ○ Dinner on Sunday is a <u>great</u> meal.

2. ○ Mom bakes <u>fresh</u> bread.
   ○ Mom <u>bakes</u> fresh bread.
   ○ Mom bakes fresh <u>bread.</u>

3. ○ <u>Dad</u> makes spicy stew.
   ○ Dad makes <u>spicy</u> stew.
   ○ Dad <u>makes</u> spicy stew.

4. ○ I pour glasses of <u>cold</u> milk.
   ○ I <u>pour</u> glasses of cold milk.
   ○ I pour <u>glasses</u> of cold milk.

5. ○ Sweet oranges <u>are</u> our dessert.
   ○ <u>Sweet</u> oranges are our dessert.
   ○ Sweet <u>oranges</u> are our dessert.

6. ○ <u>We</u> wash the dirty dishes together.
   ○ We <u>wash</u> the dirty dishes together.
   ○ We wash the <u>dirty</u> dishes together.

Home Activity Your child prepared for taking tests on adjectives for what kind. Together read a short, simple newspaper or magazine article. Have your child circle adjectives that tell what kind.

Adjectives for What Kind

Circle the adjective that tells what kind.

1. pretty robe

2. sad song

3. long poem

4. warm cake

5. busy city

Choose the adjective in ( ) that completes each sentence correctly.
Write the adjective on the line.

6. The _____ moon shines.
   (messy, bright)

7. The _____ children laugh.
   (happy, deep)

8. They write poems on _____ paper.
   (sleepy, clean)

© Pearson Education

Home Activity Your child reviewed adjectives for what kind. Write *cat, door, lemon, table* on paper. Ask
your child to write adjectives that tell what kind go with each noun (examples: *hungry cat, open door,
sour lemon, wooden table*).

Grammar and Writing Practice Book

Adjectives for How Many

Some **adjectives** tell how many.

one baby   **three** dogs

Draw lines to match the words to the pictures.

1. two cribs.

2. four chairs

3. five pictures

4. three boys

5. one house

Home Activity Your child learned about adjectives for how many. Read a counting story with your child. Have your child point out the adjectives that tell how many and use his or her fingers to show how many each adjective describes.

Name _____

Adjectives for How Many

Look at the picture.
Complete each sentence with
an adjective from the box.

| one | two | three |

1. There are _____ people in this family.

2. There are _____ children.

3. There is _____ man.

Write about the people in your family.
Use adjectives that tell how many.

_____
_____
_____
_____
_____

Home Activity Your child learned how to use adjectives for how many in writing. Place groups of one, two, three, four, and five pennies on a table and have your child write sentences about the groups using adjectives that tell how many.

Adjectives for How Many

Mark the sentence that has a line under the adjective.

1. ○ There are <u>ten</u> families in the park.
   ○ There are ten <u>families</u> in the park.
   ○ There are ten families in the <u>park</u>.

2. ○ Four brothers <u>throw</u> a football.
   ○ Four brothers throw a <u>football</u>.
   ○ <u>Four</u> brothers throw a football.

3. ○ I see three <u>fathers</u> on a bench.
   ○ I see <u>three</u> fathers on a bench.
   ○ I <u>see</u> three fathers on a bench.

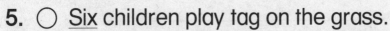

4. ○ Where <u>are</u> my two sisters?
   ○ Where are my two <u>sisters</u>?
   ○ Where are my <u>two</u> sisters?

5. ○ <u>Six</u> children play tag on the grass.
   ○ Six children <u>play</u> tag on the grass.
   ○ Six children play tag on the <u>grass</u>.

6. ○ There are five <u>mothers</u> with babies.
   ○ There are <u>five</u> mothers with babies.
   ○ There are five mothers with <u>babies</u>.

Home Activity Your child prepared for taking tests on adjectives for how many. Together read a short, simple newspaper or magazine article. Have your child circle adjectives that tell how many.

© Pearson Education

Adjectives for How Many

Circle the adjective that tells how many.

1. Mom rocks one baby.

2. Dad paints two chairs.

3. Peter stacks ten blocks.

Choose the correct adjective from the box.
Write the adjective on the line.

two	three	four

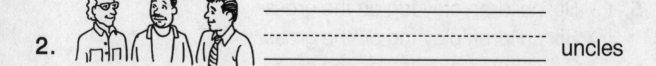

1. _____ aunts

2. _____ uncles

3. _____ cousins

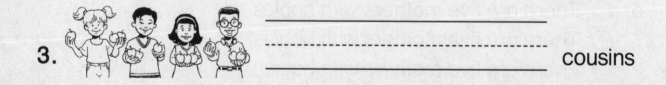

Home Activity Your child reviewed adjectives for how many. Say words such as *boxes*, *children*, *ducks*, and *books*. Have your child add an adjective that tells how many and use both the noun and the adjective in a sentence.

Grammar and Writing Practice Book

© Pearson Education

Adjectives That Compare

Add **-er** to an adjective to compare
two persons, places, or things.

    The cat is **smaller** than the dog.

Add **-est** to an adjective to compare
three or more persons, places, or things.

    The mouse is **smallest** of the three.

Circle the adjectives that compare two things.
Underline the adjectives that compare three or more things.

1. Mrs. Hopper is taller than Henry.

2. Henry's father is tallest of the three.

3. Mudge is smarter than that dog.

4. Mudge is the smartest dog of all.

5. Henry's mother is older than Henry.

6. Mrs. Hopper is oldest of the three.

Home Activity Your child learned about adjectives that compare. Read a story with your child. Have your child look for adjectives that compare and tell what things are being compared.

Adjectives That Compare

Write about three special friends.
Use words from the box or your own
adjectives that compare.

oldest	shorter	quieter	faster	tallest

_____

- -

_____

- -

_____

- -

_____

- -

_____

- -

_____

- -

_____

© Pearson Education

Home Activity Your child learned how to use adjectives that compare in writing. Talk about neighbors
or family friends with your child. Together write sentences that compare two or more of these people.
Use an adjective with *-er* or *-est* in each sentence.

Grammar and Writing Practice Book

Adjectives That Compare

Mark the sentence that has a line under the adjective.

1. ○ Ms. Feld's lawn is <u>greener</u> than Mrs. Ho's lawn.
   ○ Ms. Feld's <u>lawn</u> is greener than Mrs. Ho's lawn.
   ○ Ms. Feld's lawn <u>is</u> greener than Mrs. Ho's lawn.

2. ○ <u>Mr. Jones</u> has the brownest lawn of all.
   ○ Mr. Jones <u>has</u> the brownest lawn of all.
   ○ Mr. Jones has the <u>brownest</u> lawn of all.

3. ○ Mr. Wyner's <u>trees</u> are shorter than Mrs. Garcia's trees.
   ○ Mr. Wyner's trees are <u>shorter</u> than Mrs. Garcia's trees.
   ○ Mr. Wyner's trees <u>are</u> shorter than Mrs. Garcia's trees.

4. ○ Mr. Scott has the tallest <u>trees</u> in the neighborhood.
   ○ Mr. Scott has the tallest trees in the <u>neighborhood</u>.
   ○ Mr. Scott has the <u>tallest</u> trees in the neighborhood.

5. ○ Our house is <u>older</u> than Mrs. Vin's house.
   ○ Our <u>house</u> is older than Mrs. Vin's house.
   ○ Our house is older <u>than</u> Mrs. Vin's house.

6. ○ <u>Dr. Ruiz</u> owns the newest house on our street.
   ○ Dr. Ruiz owns the <u>newest</u> house on our street.
   ○ Dr. Ruiz owns the newest house on our <u>street</u>.

Home Activity Your child prepared for taking tests on adjectives that compare. With your child, look through a newspaper or magazine article. Help your child circle adjectives that compare. Then discuss what each adjective is comparing.

© Pearson Education

Adjectives That Compare

Circle each adjective that compares.
Write the adjectives in the chart.

1. My hat is warmer than your hat.

2. Jake's hat is the warmest hat of all.

3. Her shoes are smaller than his shoes.

4. The baby's shoes are the smallest shoes of all.

Adjectives with **-er**	Adjectives with **-est**

Add *-er* or *-est* to the word in ( ).
Write the new word on the line.

5. Her dress is _____ than my dress.
   (short)

6. That dress is the _____ dress.
   (long)

Home Activity Your child reviewed adjectives that compare. Write *old, new, slow, fast* on paper. Have your child add *-er* and *-est* to each word and then use each *-er* and *-est* word in a sentence.

Name _____

Commands

A **command** is a sentence that tells someone to do something. It begins with a **capital letter**. It ends with a **period** (.).

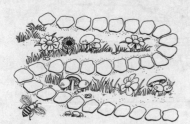

Go to the garden.

Please watch the dog.

Underline each sentence that is a command.

1. Are you thirsty?

2. Pour a glass of milk.

3. You spilled some milk.

4. Please wipe up the milk.

5. Let me help you.

6. Drink your milk.

 Home Activity Your child learned about commands. Explain how to play a game to your child. Have your child say "Command" each time he or she hears you use a command.

Commands

Pam has a problem with her cat.
What should Pam do?
Write about your ideas.
Use commands.

_____

- -

_____

- -

_____

- -

_____

- -

_____

- -

_____

- -

_____

- -

_____

- -

_____

Home Activity Your child learned how to use commands in writing. Ask your child to write about how to make a sandwich. Then have your child underline commands he or she used.

Name _____

Commands

Mark the sentence that has a command.

1. ○ Look in the newspaper.
   ○ Will you look in the newspaper?
   ○ Ben looks in the newspaper.

2. ○ Meg will find the answer.
   ○ Find the answer.
   ○ Did she find the answer?

3. ○ Cam left the key here.
   ○ Where is the key?
   ○ Please find the key.

4. ○ Will the glue hold the pieces together?
   ○ I will glue the pieces together.
   ○ Glue the pieces together.

5. ○ Who dropped the letter in the box?
   ○ Please drop the letter in the box.
   ○ Ann dropped the letter in the box.

6. ○ Look at this dirty shirt.
   ○ This shirt is dirty.
   ○ Why is this shirt dirty?

© Pearson Education

Home Activity Your child prepared for taking tests on commands. Together read a favorite story. Have your child point out commands, questions, and statements in the story.

Commands

Circle the command.
Draw a picture for the command.

1. Can you find the book?	
2. He wants the book.	
3. Show me the book.	

Underline each sentence that is a command.

4. You can help the girl.

5. Fix the car.

6. I can read the book.

7. Get the book.

8. She likes that book.

School-Home CONNECTION

Home Activity Your child reviewed commands. Take turns with your child giving each other commands about things to do in the room. For example, *Pick up that pillow. Sit in the chair. Close the door. Find a book.*

Grammar and Writing Practice Book

Exclamations

An **exclamation** is a sentence that shows strong feeling. It begins with a **capital letter**. It ends with an **exclamation mark** (!).

The kitten needs help!

Underline each sentence that is an exclamation.

1. The poor kitten is crying!

2. It must be lost!

3. Where does it live?

4. I will find its home.

5. Now the kitten is happy!

6. We can have fun now!

Home Activity Your child learned about exclamations. Have your child read each exclamation on this page with strong feeling. Then take turns with your child saying exclamations of your own.

© Pearson Education

Exclamations

How did you help someone or something?
Write about what you did.
Use an exclamation to show how you felt.

_____
- - - - - - - - - - - - - - - -
_____

_____
- - - - - - - - - - - - - - - -
_____

_____
- - - - - - - - - - - - - - - -
_____

_____
- - - - - - - - - - - - - - - -
_____

_____
- - - - - - - - - - - - - - - -
_____

School-Home CONNECTION

Home Activity Your child learned how to use exclamations in writing. Name an object in the room and a word that describes the object *(lamp/bright; sofa/big; pillow/soft; rug/dark)*. Have your child write exclamations using the word pairs *(The lamp is too bright! That pillow is so soft!)*.

Exclamations

Mark the correct exclamation.

1. ○ the baby bird cannot fly!
   ○ The baby bird cannot fly!
   ○ The baby bird cannot fly

2. ○ The bird is so small!
   ○ The bird is so small
   ○ the bird is so small!

3. ○ mole loves the bird!
   ○ Mole loves the bird
   ○ Mole loves the bird!

4. ○ I can't wait to see Grandpa!
   ○ I can't wait to see Grandpa
   ○ I can't wait to see Grandpa?

5. ○ grandpa is so wise!
   ○ Grandpa is so wise!
   ○ Grandpa is so wise

6. ○ Oh no, the bird fell from its nest
   ○ oh no, the bird fell from its nest!
   ○ Oh no, the bird fell from its nest!

© Pearson Education

Home Activity Your child prepared for taking tests on exclamations. Together read a favorite book. Have your child point out the exclamations and tell how he or she knew they were exclamations.

Exclamations

Read each pair of sentences.
Write the exclamation on the line.

1. Hal is so sad! His dog Rip ran away.

_____
- -
_____

2. Where is Rip? Hal looks everywhere!

_____
- -
_____

3. Hal hears a sound. Rip is back!

_____
- -
_____

Write each exclamation correctly.

4. hal is so happy

_____
- -
_____

5. rip is the best dog of all

_____
- -
_____

School-Home CONNECTION

Home Activity Your child reviewed exclamations. With your child, look through newspaper and magazine ads. Have your child highlight the exclamations he or she finds.

Grammar and Writing Practice Book

How Sentences Begin and End

A **sentence** is a group of words that tells a complete idea. It begins with a **capital letter**. A statement ends with a **period** (.).
A question ends with a **question mark** (?).

What animal is Dot**?**

He is a mouse**.**

Circle each group of words that is a
complete sentence and is written correctly.

I. What do they want?

2. Solve a mystery?

3. They find a mystery.

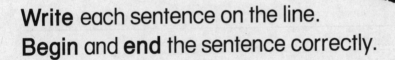

Write each sentence on the line.
Begin and **end** the sentence correctly.

4. acorns come from oak trees

_____

- -

_____

5. where is the oak tree

_____

- -

_____

School-Home
CONNECTION

Home Activity Your child learned about how sentences begin and end. Ask your child questions about objects in the room. Have your child answer using complete sentences.

Dot & Jabber

APPLY TO WRITING

How Sentences Begin and End

Write each sentence correctly.

1. do they solve the mystery

   _____
   -
   _____

2. they find the answer

   _____
   -
   _____

Write sentences about a problem you solved.
Tell what the problem was.
Tell what you did.

   _____
   -
   _____

   _____
   -
   _____

   _____
   -
   _____

   _____
   -
   _____

Home Activity Your child learned how to begin and end sentences in writing. Copy simple sentences from a story, but leave off the capital letters at the beginning and the punctuation at the end. Have your child write the sentences correctly.

How Sentences Begin and End

Mark the group of words that is a complete sentence and is written correctly.

1. ○ Little oak tree from an acorn.
   ○ the little oak tree grew from an acorn.
   ○ The little oak tree grew from an acorn.

2. ○ Is the big oak tree across the meadow?
   ○ The big oak tree the meadow?
   ○ is the big oak tree across the meadow?

3. ○ The mole in a hole.
   ○ The mole lives in a hole.
   ○ the mole lives in a hole.

4. ○ Dot and Jabber look for clues.
   ○ Dot and Jabber.
   ○ dot and Jabber look for clues.

5. ○ Why does the squirrel?
   ○ Why does the squirrel want the acorn?
   ○ The squirrel want the acorn?

6. ○ The acorn in a hole.
   ○ the squirrel hides the acorn in a hole.
   ○ The squirrel hides the acorn in a hole.

Home Activity Your child prepared for taking tests on how sentences begin and end. Together read a favorite storybook. Have your child point out statements and questions and explain how they are alike and different.

How Sentences Begin and End

Circle each group of words that is a complete sentence.

1. Dot and Jabber are detectives.

2. Like a good mystery

3. Why is the oak tree here?

4. that mystery.

5. They will find out.

Change each statement to a question. **Write** the new sentence on the line. An example is in the box below.

The tree is growing.	Is the tree growing?

6. Dot is looking for clues.

_____
- -
_____

7. He will look in the hole.

_____
- -
_____

8. The mole is angry.

_____
- -
_____

Home Activity Your child reviewed how sentences begin and end. Have your child write a sentence about something he or she likes to do.

© Pearson Education

Pronouns

A **pronoun** is a word that takes the place of a noun or nouns. The words **he, she, it, we, you**, and **they** are pronouns.

Levers are simple machines.
Jake uses a lever.

They are simple machines.
He uses a lever.

Circle the pronoun in each sentence.

1. We use machines every day.

2. They make work easier.

3. She will use a lever.

4. Will it open a bottle?

Circle the pronoun in ( ) that takes the place of the underlined word or words.

1. This box is heavy. (She, It)

2. Tina and I set up a ramp. (He, We)

3. Jim puts the box on the ramp. (He, They)

4. Tina and Jim push the box up the ramp. (They, You)

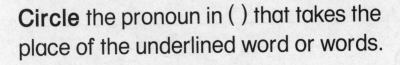

Home Activity Your child learned about pronouns. Write *he, she, it, we, you,* and *they* in a list. Point to each word and ask your child to use it in a sentence.

© Pearson Education

Pronouns

Look at the picture.
Write about what the people are doing.
Use pronouns.

_____

- - - - - - - - - - - - - - - - - -

_____

- - - - - - - - - - - - - - - - - -

_____

- - - - - - - - - - - - - - - - - -

_____

- - - - - - - - - - - - - - - - - -

_____

- - - - - - - - - - - - - - - - - -

_____

- - - - - - - - - - - - - - - - - -

_____

Home Activity Your child learned how to use pronouns in writing. With your child, look through a family photo album. Talk about what you see in the photos using pronouns instead of names.

Grammar and Writing Practice Book

Pronouns

Mark the pronoun that can replace each underlined word or words.

1. <u>Simple machines</u> have few parts.
   - ○ **A** He
   - ○ **B** It
   - ○ **C** They

2. <u>An inclined plane</u> is a simple machine.
   - ○ **A** It
   - ○ **B** She
   - ○ **C** You

3. <u>Maria and I</u> ride on a seesaw.
   - ○ **A** It
   - ○ **B** We
   - ○ **C** She

4. <u>Karen</u> has two wheels on her bike.
   - ○ **A** She
   - ○ **B** They
   - ○ **C** We

5. <u>George</u> can ride on one wheel.
   - ○ **A** They
   - ○ **B** He
   - ○ **C** It

Home Activity Your child prepared for taking tests on pronouns. Together look through a newspaper or magazine article. Take turns finding and circling the pronouns *he, she, it, we, you,* and *they.*

Name _____

Pronouns

Circle the pronoun in each sentence.

1. You can use a pulley.

2. It can lift a heavy box.

3. He has a wheelbarrow.

4. We will move the plants.

5. Are they ready?

Change the underlined word or words to a pronoun from the box. Write the new sentence on the line.

He	They	She

6. <u>Ann and Ed</u> want a garden.

_____

- -

_____

7. <u>Ann</u> digs holes.

_____

- -

_____

8. <u>Ed</u> puts in seeds.

_____

- -

_____

Home Activity Your child reviewed pronouns. Copy sentences that have nouns as subjects from a favorite storybook. Have your child write the sentences using pronouns in place of the nouns.

Name _____

Using *I* and *Me*

The pronouns **I** and **me** take the place of your name. Use **I** in the subject of a sentence. Use **me** after an action verb. Always write **I** with a capital letter.

Rosa calls **me**. I talk to her.

When you talk about yourself and another person, name yourself last. The pronouns **I** and **me** take the place of your name.

Cal and **I** talk on the phone. Rosa calls Cal and **me**.

_____

Write *I* or *me* to complete each sentence.

1. _____ see an old basket.

2. It gives _____ an idea.

3. _____ take the basket home.

4. Rosa and _____ paint it.

5. See Rosa and _____ put our socks in it!

Home Activity Your child learned about using *I* and *me*. Take turns telling about ways you use the telephone. Use *I* and *me* as you talk.

Alexander Graham Bell

APPLY TO WRITING

Using *I* and *Me*

Write about the best thing you have ever made.
It might be a toy, a food, or a gift.
Use *I* and *me*.

_____

- -

_____

- -

_____

- -

_____

- -

_____

- -

_____

- -

_____

- -

_____

© Pearson Education

School-Home CONNECTION

Home Activity Your child learned how to use *I* and *me* in writing. Have your child read aloud the story he or she wrote on this page. Ask your child to point out the *I*'s and *me*'s.

Grammar and Writing Practice Book

Using *I* and *Me*

Mark the letter of the word or words that complete each sentence.

1. ____ invented a new food.
   - ○ **A** Dad and me
   - ○ **B** Dad and I
   - ○ **C** Me

2. ____ call it Crunch Surprise.
   - ○ **A** Me
   - ○ **B** Dad and me
   - ○ **C** I

3. Dad gives ____ a bowl.
   - ○ **A** Mom and me
   - ○ **B** Mom and I
   - ○ **C** I

4. ____ love the taste.
   - ○ **A** Mom and me
   - ○ **B** Me
   - ○ **C** Mom and I

5. Crunch Surprise makes ____ proud.
   - ○ **A** I
   - ○ **B** Dad and me
   - ○ **C** Dad and I

Home Activity Your child prepared for taking tests on using *I* and *me*. Ask your child to read the sentences on this page and to say the word or words that complete each sentence as he or she reads.

Using *I* and *Me*

Write *I* or *me* to complete each sentence.
Circle the picture that answers the riddle.

1. _____ am small.

2. Hear _____ ring.

3. What am _____ ?

Write the word in ( ) that completes each sentence.

4. Bill gives _____ some wood. (I, me).

5. _____ make a chair for my doll. (I, me)

6. Now Nell and _____ both have chairs. (I, me)

Home Activity Your child reviewed using *I* and *me*. Ask your child to make up another riddle using the riddle on this page as a model. Make sure your child includes the words *I* and *me* in the riddle.

More About Pronouns

A **pronoun** can take the place of some words in a sentence. **I, you, he, she, it, we,** and **they** are used in the **naming part** of a sentence. **Me, you, him, her, it, us,** and **them** are used in the **action part** of a sentence.

> **Ben** makes **kites. He** makes **them.**

Write the pronoun in ( ) that can take the place of the underlined word or words.

1. <u>Ben</u> works in a shop. (Him, He) _____

2. <u>Candles</u> are lit. (They, Them) _____

3. Ben tells <u>his mother.</u> (she, her) _____

4. The kite pulls <u>Ben.</u> (he, him) _____

5. Ben amazes <u>his friends.</u> (them, they) _____

6. I like <u>Ben's idea.</u> (her, it) _____

Home Activity Your child learned more about pronouns. Ask your child to make up new sentences using the pronouns he or she wrote on this page.

More About Pronouns

Imagine you are at the pond when Ben flies his kite.

Write about what happens. **Use** the pronouns *it, he, him, I, me, we,* or *us.*

_____

- -

_____

- -

_____

- -

_____

- -

_____

- -

_____

- -

_____

Home Activity Your child learned how to use pronouns in writing. Take turns with your child writing sentences using the pronouns listed on this page.

More About Pronouns

Mark the pronoun that can replace the underlined word or words.

1. The young boy has many ideas.
   - ○ He
   - ○ Them
   - ○ We

2. His father asks <u>Ben</u> about his plan.
   - ○ he
   - ○ she
   - ○ him

3. Ben needs <u>a strong wind</u>.
   - ○ him
   - ○ it
   - ○ you

4. <u>Ben's friends</u> wonder about the kite.
   - ○ Them
   - ○ He
   - ○ They

5. His plan surprises <u>the boys</u>.
   - ○ them
   - ○ they
   - ○ we

Home Activity Your child prepared for taking tests on pronouns. Read aloud a favorite storybook to your child. Ask your child to say "Stop" each time he or she hears a pronoun and to identify the pronoun.

School-Home
CONNECTION

© Pearson Education

More About Pronouns

Write the pronoun from the box that can replace the underlined word or words.

her	him	it

1. Omar has <u>a plan</u>.

_____

2. Jill will help <u>Omar</u>.

_____

3. Omar tells <u>Jill</u> his idea.

_____

Change the underlined word or words to a pronoun in ( ).
Write the new sentence.

4. <u>Omar and Jill</u> work hard. (Him, They)

_____

5. <u>Omar</u> pushes the button. (We, He)

_____

6. <u>The light</u> works! (It, They)

_____

Home Activity Your child reviewed more about pronouns. Find an article in a newspaper or magazine. Ask your child to look for and circle the pronouns in the article.

Sentences

Underline each sentence.

1. The dog needs a bath.

   The dog

2. in the tub

   The dog is in the tub.

3. The dog is too big.

   too big

Find the sentence. **Write** the sentence.

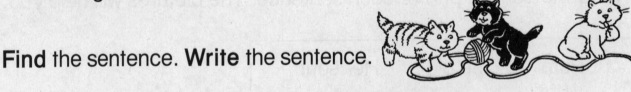

4. I see three kittens.   three kittens

   _____

   -

   _____

5. with a string   Two kittens play with a string.

   _____

   -

   _____

6. One kitten is under the bed.   is under the bed

   _____

   -

   _____

Name _____

Naming Parts of Sentences

Underline the naming part of each sentence.

1. Our cat is sick.

2. My dad takes her to the vet.

3. The vet gives her a shot.

Write the naming part of each sentence. The pictures will help you.

Pam	The pig	Her soup

4. _____ has a cold.

5. _____ makes hot soup.

6. _____ tastes good!

Action Parts of Sentences

Underline the action part of each sentence.

1. Ox helps Mom and Pop.

2. He digs in the ground.

3. He puts cans in a sack.

Write the action part of each sentence. The pictures will help you.

eat the food	rubs on Jim	feeds the cats

4. A cat _____ .

5. Jim _____ .

6. The cats _____ .

© Pearson Education

Word Order

Finish each sentence. **Use** the two words in ( ).
The picture will help you.

1. _____ watches the _____ .
   (foxes, Ann)

2. The _____ eats the _____ .
   (kit, food)

Write the words so they are in the right order.
End each sentence with a period.

3. Nap a take foxes the.

   _____

   _____

4. Fixes man the dinner.

   _____

   _____

5. Eat foxes will the.

   _____

   _____

© Pearson Education

Grammar and Writing Practice Book

Telling Sentences

Underline the sentence that is right.

1. kim saw a squirrel

   Kim saw a squirrel.

2. It was in the tree.

   it was in the tree

3. the squirrel ran away

   The squirrel ran away.

Write each sentence correctly.

4. he sees a frog

   _____

   - - - - - - - - - - - - - - - - - -

   _____

5. it is in the grass

   _____

   - - - - - - - - - - - - - - - - - -

   _____

6. the frog is green

   _____

   - - - - - - - - - - - - - - - - - -

   _____

Questions

Write each question.

1. Is this an animal park?   This is an animal park.

_____

- -

_____

2. I like zebras.   Do you like zebras?

_____

- -

_____

3. Can you see them?   I can see them.

_____

- -

_____

Look at the words. **Put** them in order to write a question.
Begin and **end** each question correctly.

4. the lion who sees

_____

- -

_____

5. the hippo where is

_____

- -

_____

Grammar and Writing Practice Book

Nouns

Write the noun for each picture.

1.   mom   dog

_____

- - - - - - - - - - - - - - - -

_____

2.   shop   park

_____

- - - - - - - - - - - - - - - -

_____

3.   dog   cat

_____

- - - - - - - - - - - - - - - -

_____

4.   ship   ball

_____

- - - - - - - - - - - - - - - -

_____

Finish each sentence.
Write a noun from the box.

boy   girl

_____

- - - - - - - - - - - - - - - -

5. The _____ runs on sand.

_____

- - - - - - - - - - - - - - - -

6. The _____ builds a castle.

Name _____

Proper Nouns

Correct each name. **Write** the name on the line.

1. max

_____

2. mopsy

_____

3. main street

_____

4. cole park

_____

Write the sentences.
Use a capital letter for each proper noun.

5. Is dave the farmer?

_____

----

6. Does beth make a mask?

_____

© Pearson Education

Grammar and Writing Practice Book

Special Titles

Write the title and the name correctly on the line.

1. dr. flores

_____

- -

_____

2. miss simon

_____

- -

_____

3. mr. caine

_____

- -

_____

Write each sentence.
Use capital letters and periods correctly.

4. ms gorski is our teacher.

_____

- -

_____

5. dr merck is a vet.

_____

- -

_____

Days, Months, and Holidays

Write the day, month, or holiday correctly on the line.

1. The neighbors have a block party in may.

_____

- -

_____

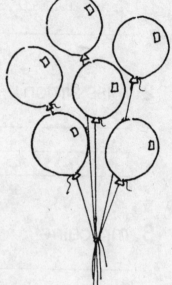

2. The block party is on memorial day.

_____

- -

_____

3. The holiday is on monday.

_____

- -

_____

Match the words to the clues.
Write each word correctly.

| thanksgiving | friday | october |

_____

- -

4. holiday _____

_____

- -

5. day _____

_____

- -

6. month _____

One and More Than One

Draw a line from the picture to the correct noun.

1.  bird

birds

2.  bear

bears

3. 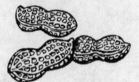 nut

nuts

4.  rock

rocks

Finish the sentences.
Write the correct word on the line.

5. The plant has one _____ .

(flower, flowers)

6. Two _____ are by the pond.

(frog, frogs)

© Pearson Education

Name _____

Nouns in Sentences

Circle the two nouns in each sentence.

1. The queen rules the hive.

2. Workers do the jobs.

3. Flowers have sweet nectar.

4. Honey is in the cells.

5. A bear makes the bees mad.

Finish the sentences.

Write a noun from the box.

drones	Ann	tree

6. The hive is in a _____ .

7. The _____ help the queen.

8. Does _____ like bees?

Grammar and Writing Practice Book

Action Verbs

Circle the verb in each sentence.

1. Leaves fall from the trees.

2. The wind blows the leaves.

3. Pat dances with the leaves.

Circle the correct verb in ( ) to complete each sentence.
Write the verb on the line.

4. The sun _____ at six.
   (sets, runs)

5. The moon _____ at night.
   (plays, shines)

6. May _____ in her bed.
   (sleeps, barks)

Verbs That Add -s

Complete the sentences. **Write** the correct verb on the line.

1. The kitten _____ under the bed.
   (hides, hide)

2. The cat _____ the kitten.
   (lick, licks)

3. Fluffy _____ over the fence.
   (leaps, leap)

Add -s to the verb in ( ) to complete each sentence.
Write the verb on the line.

4. The baby _____ on the floor. (crawl)

5. The girl _____ with the cat. (play)

6. Ms. Chou _____ dinner. (cook)

Verbs That Do Not Add -s

Circle the verb that shows more than one.

1. Meg and Jen (moves, move) away.

2. They (pack, packs) their things.

3. The girls (feels, feel) sad.

Circle the correct verb. Write the verb on the line.

_____
- -
4. Pat and Jim _____ the new girls.

                (sees, see)

_____
- -
5. The boys _____ to Meg and Jen.

            (talk, talks)

_____
- -
6. They _____ games with them.

       (plays, play)

Now and the Past

Read each word in the box. **Write** the word under *Now* if it tells about now. **Write** the word under *The Past* if it tells about the past.

likes	asked	planted
shouted	jumps	looks

Now   **The Past**

1. _____   4. _____

2. _____   5. _____

3. _____   6. _____

Complete each sentence. **Write** the correct verb on the line.

7. Yesterday Toad _____ a garden.
   (wanted, wants)

8. Today Frog _____ Toad.
   (helps, helped)

Name _____

Am, Is, Are, Was, and Were

Circle the verb in each sentence. **Write** *Now* if the sentence tells about now. **Write** *Past* if the sentence tells about the past.

1. I am a caterpillar. _____

2. I was hungry. _____

3. Leaves are good! _____

Choose the correct verb in ( ) to complete the sentence. **Write** the verb on the line.

4. A pupa _____ soft.
    (am, is)

5. Eggs _____ hard.
    (is, are)

6. The wings _____ wet.
    (were, was)

Grammar and Writing Practice Book

Contractions with *Not*

Draw a line from the words to their contraction.

1. are not   doesn't

2. does not   isn't

3. do not   weren't

4. is not   aren't

5. were not   don't

Write the contraction for the underlined words.

6. The bear <u>is not</u> eating now.   _____

7. The raccoons <u>were not</u> going away.   _____

8. Geese <u>do not</u> wait for snow.   _____

9. Days <u>are not</u> warm in the winter.   _____

10. A squirrel <u>does not</u> mind the cold.   _____

Grammar and Writing Practice Book

Adjectives

Circle the adjective. Write the adjective on the line.

1. hot stove _____

2. best friends _____

3. big present _____

Complete each sentence.
Write an adjective from the box.

tall	old	tiny

4. Ted likes _____ books.

5. Dot has _____ cups.

6. Jen loves _____ flowers.

Adjectives for Colors and Shapes

Circle the adjective in each sentence that names a color or shape.

1. Sara paints on square paper.

2. Here is blue water.

3. There are yellow fish.

4. Gray whales swim by.

5. White birds fly over.

Choose the adjective in ( ).
Write the adjective on the line.

6. Dad cooks _____ beans.
   (black, clock)

7. He stirs in _____ peppers.
   (rip, red)

8. He pours soup into _____ bowls.
   (round, frown)

© Pearson Education

Adjectives for Sizes

Circle the adjective that describes size.

1. long snake

2. big book

3. little cat

Look at the pictures. **Write** the adjective in ( ) that tells about each picture.

4. _____ ring
   (short, small)

5. _____ whale
   (tiny, huge)

6. _____ tree
   (tall, lazy)

© Pearson Education

Name _____

Adjectives for What Kind

Circle the adjective that tells what kind.

1. hard piñata

2. heavy stick

3. fast child

4. funny toys

5. sweet treats

Choose the adjective in ( ) that completes each sentence correctly. **Write** the adjective on the line.

6. Rosa had a _____ party.
(great, sour)

7. She wore a _____ dress.
(sad, fancy)

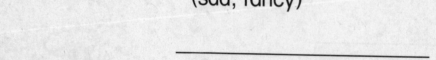

8. The band played _____ music.
(open, loud)

Name _____

Adjectives for How Many

Circle the adjective that tells how many.

1. Peter has four aunts.

2. Does Jane have five uncles?

3. Six cousins came to my house.

Choose the correct adjective from the box.
Write the adjective on the line.

one	two	three

4.  _____ brothers

5.  _____ sisters

6.  _____ dad

Adjectives That Compare

Circle each adjective that compares.
Write the adjectives in the chart.

1. Is this scarf shorter than that one?

2. Jan has the longest scarf of all.

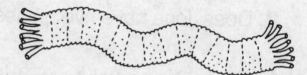

3. Ted's coat is longer than my coat.

4. Who has the shortest coat of all?

Adjectives with *-er*	Adjectives with *-est*

Add *-er* to the word in ( ).
Write the new word on the line.

5. My jacket is _____ than your coat.
   (light)

6. His boots are _____ than her shoes.
   (thick)

Commands

Underline each sentence that is a command.

1. This shirt needs a button.

2. Please find a needle.

3. Hand me the thread.

4. Where is the button?

Write each command correctly.

5. help me thread the needle

_____

- -

_____

6. put the button here

_____

- -

_____

7. please sew it on the shirt

_____

- -

_____

8. stitch it neatly

_____

- -

_____

Exclamations

Read each pair of sentences. **Write** the exclamation on the line.

1. Where is the bird? It fell from the nest!

   _____
   -
   _____

2. The bird needs help! Mole takes it home.

   _____
   -
   _____

3. Grandpa talks to Mole. The bird is so sad!

   _____
   -
   _____

Write each exclamation correctly.

4. that bird flies fast

   _____
   -
   _____

5. it must be miles away

   _____
   -
   _____

How Sentences Begin and End

Write each sentence on the line. **Begin** and **end** the sentence correctly.

1. can an acorn fly

   _____

   -

   _____

2. the acorn did not walk

   _____

   -

   _____

3. how did it get here

   _____

   -

   _____

Change each statement to a question. **Write** the new sentence on the line. An example is in the box below.

They are walking.	Are they walking?

4. Maple seeds are twirling.

   _____

   -

   _____

5. They will ride on the wind.

   _____

   -

   _____

Pronouns

Circle the pronoun in each sentence.

1. Do you use simple machines?

2. He uses a lever every day.

3. It opens the door.

4. Can we think of more simple machines?

Circle the pronoun in ( ) that takes the place of the underlined word or words.

5. Wheels help a car move. (They, He)

6. A pulley raises the sail on a boat. (We, It)

7. The girl pushes the wheelbarrow. (She, They)

8. The boy moves the heavy rock. (You, He)

© Pearson Education

Using *I* and *Me*

Write *I* or *me* to complete each sentence.

1. Mom gives _____ some tape.

2. The tape and _____ are stuck.

3. _____ will invent new tape!

Choose the word in ( ) that completes each sentence.
Write the sentence.

4. Kai and ____ made a robot. (I, me)

_____

_____

5. It brings ____ my book. (I, me)

_____

_____

6. It helps Kai and ____. (I, me)

_____

_____

Name _____

More About Pronouns

Write the pronoun from the box that can replace the underlined word or words.

it   them   her

1. Joe shows <u>Rita</u> a hat.

_____

2. Joe invented <u>the hat</u>.

_____

3. Rita does not like <u>hats</u>.

_____

Change the underlined word or words to a pronoun. **Write** the new sentence.

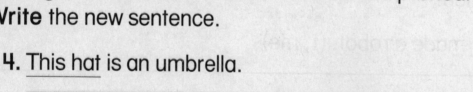

4. <u>This hat</u> is an umbrella.

_____
_____

5. <u>Rita and her friends</u> like the hat.

_____
_____

6. Rita asks <u>Joe</u> for more hats.

_____
_____

Grammar and Writing Practice Book

Name _____

Story Chart

Fill out this story chart to help you organize your ideas.

Title _____

Beginning

Middle

End

© Pearson Education

Name _____

Use Words That Tell How You Feel

Write a word from the box to tell how the writer feels.

Use each word one time. The pictures will help you.

Word Bank
happy
sad
scared
mad

1. My brother took my book.

    _____

    I feel _____.

2. I won a prize.

    _____

    I feel _____.

3. My best friend moved away.

    _____

    I feel _____.

4. A dog growled at me.

    _____

    I feel _____.

© Pearson Education

Name _____

Writing Trait: Voice

Which sentence in each pair tells how the writer feels?

Underline the sentence.

1. I eat an apple at lunch every day.

   I just love a crisp, sweet apple!

2. I have the smartest dog in the world!

   I have a dog.

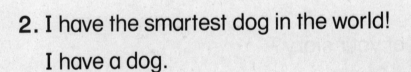

3. I have a part in the school play.

   I have a million butterflies in my stomach!

4. Joe is my friend.

   Joe tells the funniest jokes!

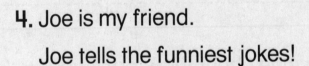

5. I like loud, exciting movies!

   I saw a movie last weekend.

Name _____

Self-Evaluation Guide

Check *Yes* or *No* about voice in your story.

	Yes	No
I. I used words that tell how I feel.		
2. I used one or more words that describe.		
3. I used one or more words that show action.		

Answer the questions.

4. What is the best part of your story?

_____

----

5. What is one thing you would change about this story if you could write it again?

_____

Name _____

How-to Chart

Fill out this how-to chart to help you organize your ideas.

Title _____

Step 1

Step 2

Step 3

Name _____

Time-Order Words

Number the steps in order.
Add a time-order word from the box to
each sentence.
Write the sentences in order.

_____ Bees get nectar from the flowers.

_____ Bees make honey from the nectar.

_____ Bees fly to flowers.

_____
- -
_____

_____
- -
_____

_____
- -
_____

© Pearson Education

Name _____

Writing Trait: Order

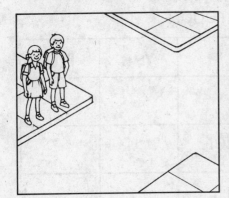  

Look at the pictures.

Write these three sentences in the right order.

The children cross the street.
The children wait.
The woman stops the cars.

1. _____

2. _____

3. _____

Write a sentence that tells what could happen next.

4. _____

Name _____

Self-Evaluation Guide

Check *Yes* or *No* about order in your how-to report.

	Yes	No
1. I wrote the steps in the correct order.		
2. I used one or more words to show the order.		
3. I used one or more words that show action.		

Answer the questions.

4. What is the best part of your how-to report?

_____

_____

_____

_____

5. What is one thing you would change about this how-to report if you could write it again?

_____

_____

_____

Name _____

Details Web

Fill out this details web to help you organize your ideas.

Name _____

Strong Verbs

Look at the verbs in dark type.
Which sentence in each pair has a stronger verb?
Underline the sentence.

1. The boys **race** to the park.

   The boys **go** to the park.

2. Dan **says**, "Look at me!"

   Dan **shouts**, "Look at me!"

3. She **put** flowers in the garden.

   She **planted** flowers in the garden.

4. Ann **cuts** a rose from the bush.

   Ann **gets** a rose from the bush.

5. They **make** a birdhouse.

   They **build** a birdhouse.

Name _____

Writing Trait: Focus/Ideas

Which sentence in each group does NOT belong?
Draw a line through the sentence.

1. Many flowers bloom in spring.
   Flowers can be many colors.
   My favorite color is blue.
   Some flowers bloom in summer.

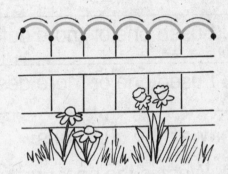

2. Andy is six years old.
   My name is Beth.
   He can ride a bike.
   He can write his name.

Finish the sentence below.
Write another sentence about this idea.

I can _____

_____

_____

_____

Name _____

Self-Evaluation Guide

Check *Yes* or *No* about focus/ideas in your description.

	Yes	No
I. All my sentences tell about my topic.		
2. I used one or more action words.		
3. I used one or more describing words.		

Answer the questions.

4. What is the best part of your description?

_____

_____

_____

_____

5. What is one thing you would change about this description if
you could write it again?

_____

_____

_____

_____

Name _____

Persuasion Chart

Fill out this persuasion chart to help you organize your ideas.

Topic I want _____ to _____.
                     (audience)   (purpose)

Brainstorm reasons here.

_____

_____

_____

_____

_____

_____

_____

Organize your reasons here.

Least important   Most important

_____   _____

_____   _____

_____   _____

Name _____

Persuasive Words

Use words from the box to complete
the letter.

Word Bank
important
best
should

April 14, 2007

Dear Doctor Lee,

_____

You _____ give an award to Mr. Vaca.

_____

He is the _____ teacher at Lane School.

_____

We learn _____ facts about our Earth from him.

Sincerely,

The First Graders

Name _____

Writing Trait: Word Choice

Good adjectives help make your writing interesting.

Write an adjective from the box to complete each sentence.

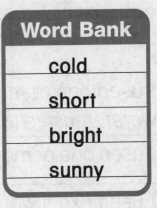

Word Bank

| cold |
| short |
| bright |
| sunny |

Dear Dad,

1–4. I think we should go to Grand Beach. You will love the

_____

warm, _____ beach. We can swim and

_____

sit under a _____ beach umbrella. We

_____

can buy _____ ice cream. The beach is

_____

just a _____ trip on the bus.

Your son,

Greg

Circle the adjective to complete each sentence.

5. Charley is a (deep, hungry) cat.

6. Ana dug a (round, sad) hole.

© Pearson Education

Name _____

Self-Evaluation Guide

Check *Yes* or *No* about word choice in your letter.

	Yes	No
1. I used one or more words to persuade (*best, worst, must, should, important, need*).		
2. I used one or more good adjectives to describe.		
3. I used exact words instead of *nice*.		

Answer the questions.

4. What is the best part of your letter?

_____

_____

_____

_____

_____

_____

_____

5. What is one thing you would change about this letter if you could write it again?

_____

_____

_____

_____

_____

_____

_____

© Pearson Education

Name _____

KWL Chart

Fill out this KWL chart to help you organize your ideas.

What We Know	What We Want to Know	What We Learned

Name _____

Eliminate Wordiness

Don't use more words than are needed.

- Take out phrases such as *kind of*, *I think that*, and *it seems like*.
- Don't use *a lot of*. Use *many* or another word.
- Don't use two words that mean the same thing: ~~great~~ big, ~~little~~ tiny.
- Don't use several words when you can use one word: moved ~~with great slowness~~, moved slowly.

Look at each pair of sentences. **Write** the words that are left out in the second sentence.

1. Dana owns a little tiny cell phone.
   Dana owns a tiny cell phone.

   _____

   -

   _____

2. It seems like Julie is kind of smart.
   Julie is smart.

   _____

   -

   _____

Look at each pair of sentences. **Write** the word that is different in the second sentence. What words did it replace?

3. Ben had a lot of great ideas.
   Ben had many great ideas.

   _____

   -

   _____

4. He carried the computer with a great deal of care.
   He carried the computer carefully.

   _____

   -

   _____

Name _____

Writing Trait: Sentences

• Use all kinds of sentences: statements, questions, commands, and exclamations.

• Use different beginnings. Don't start too many sentences with *the, he,* or *she*.

Write the letter of each sentence next to the word that identifies what kind of sentence it is.

(A) Who is Alexander Graham Bell? **(B)** He invented the telephone. **(C)** That's a wonderful invention! **(D)** Don't forget about his work with deaf people.

l. Statement: _____

2. Question: _____

3. Command: _____

4. Exclamation: _____

Rearrange the words in each sentence so it begins with the underlined word. **Write** the paragraph.

Example: She invented a new game <u>last week</u>.

Answer: Last week she invented a new game.

She played the game <u>today</u>. She changed it <u>later</u>. She likes it better <u>now</u>!

_____

_____

_____

_____

_____

Name _____

Self-Evaluation Guide

Check *Yes* or *No* about sentences in your report.

	Yes	No
1. I used facts in my research report.		
2. I used different kinds of sentences.		
3. I used different beginnings for my sentences.		

Answer the questions.

4. What is the best part of your report?

_____

_____

_____

_____

_____

5. What is one thing you would change about this report if you could write it again?

_____

_____

_____

_____

_____